Valerian Pączek: Priest, Soldier, Quiet Hero

"The cross and the sword have been symbols of the Polish soldier through the centuries."

Father Valerian Paczek

Valerian Pączek: Priest, Soldier, Quiet Hero

By William C. Sherman & John Guerrero

 University of Mary Press   Bismarck, North Dakota

Given this volume's anticipated readership and various typesetting and production restraints, the usual diacritical marks are absent from Polish and German words. In this we follow the example of Fr. Paczek himself. His name, Paczek, has a comma-like mark at the bottom of the letter "a." It should be pronounced "Pahncek," but he himself, when asked the pronunciation, replied with a smile, just like the word "paycheck."

Published by the University of Mary Press
7500 University Drive
Bismarck, ND 58504
www.umary.edu

ISBN 0-9652880-2-1

Printed in Canada

Contents

Introduction

DURING THE 1970S, the Agricultural Departments of Fargo's North Dakota State University would be hosts to a variety of agricultural professors from Poland. Leaving their wives and children at home, these scientists spent a year or more on the campus exchanging and exploring technical information with their American counterparts.

St. Paul's Newman Center, on the edge of the University complex, in a sense became their "home away from home." Students and staff welcomed them and often took them fishing or sightseeing.

Once a year, Fr. Valerian Paczek, himself of Polish background, invited them for an evening of Polish food, music, and conversation at his St. Boniface parish in Lidgerwood, North Dakota. This writer, a chaplain at the N.D.S.U. Newman Center, would accompany them on their "little touch of Poland" visits to Lidgerwood.

The two, sometimes three, gentlemen would be welcomed by Fr. Paczek with appropriate Polish salutations and soon be partaking of a familiar "old country" beverage. Some time during the festivities they would be shown about the house. At some point in the tour they would stop and stare at a rather small photograph of a uniformed Polish officer. They looked closely, observed the rank and the row of ribbons, and would swing around to look at Fr. Paczek, who admitted with a smile he was the officer in the photo. These agronomists, like many Polish professionals were themselves, for the most part, reserve officers in the modern Polish military. They knew what the ribbons and the rank stood for.

From then on the conversation centered, very often, on Poland in the Second World War: the invasions, the underground, the Uprising of 1944, and the prison camps.

This writer knew only a little of the war's events in Eastern Europe, but on each visit my ears pricked up. I heard accounts of conflict, capture, escape, and Nazi atrocities. When I returned to Fargo I would record the bits and pieces of stories, thinking that someday the notes could be of value.

For the Polish professors, this certainly was one of their big surprises in America: to find a genuine hero of their country's liberation battles, living as a parish priest in a rather small town in the middle of America!

As the years went by, my library on World War Polish events began to expand. Whenever I was in Fr. Paczek's presence, I listened carefully in case he might mention something of his war experiences. Such stories, I confess, were few and far between. His former parishioners will be the first to admit that other than knowing "he was in the war," they knew little else. Though he was the most gregarious of individuals, war seldom was part of his conversation.

Father Valerian died on June 18, 2001 at the age of 91. He was incapacitated the last several years through the effects of a stroke. The story of his life passed away with him, with the exception of one little booklet published on the fiftieth anniversary of his priestly ordination (*On the Golden Jubilee of Fr. Valerian Paczek*, Lidgerwood, N.D. 1984). This booklet contains only five pages of his early biography; rather most of the text is a salute to his four North Dakota parishes and the lively faith he found in their congregations.

One other, more valuable volume concerns his life more directly. It was written in Polish (*55 Lat W Sluzbie Bogu*, Ojczyznei i. Bliznim, Lidgerwood, N.D. 1989). Here he indicates on the title page that he is Ks Dr. Walerian Paczek, PPLK, "one time chief chaplain of the North Group in Warsaw." This book, 70 pages long, was probably written "for the record," since the Communist government in Poland was falling apart and historical research concerning the Polish non-Communist underground was beginning to be published. In these little volumes, he included numerous photos of military and ecclesiastical figures that were part of his life. In both publications, Fr. Paczek, when discussing his young life, his education, and even his war and post-war years, is extremely modest. He describes the events but seldom uses personal pronouns. His reticence is evident in his public writings and it was certainly true of his conversations with friends.

LuAnn Kuntz, in 1978, through the urging of Fr. Al Bitz, wrote a remarkable volume—*Fare Thee Well*—concerning eight priests in the Diocese of Fargo who had concentration camp or slave labor backgrounds. The booklet was well edited (the now well-known Leo Kim did the design), the Knights of Columbus sponsored it, and it stands as a tribute to the heroic priests who have now gone to their eternal reward.

Fr. Valerian Paczek is featured on two pages in the volume. LuAnn Kuntz writes: His grandfatherly smile covers a memory bank of hair-raising incidents. . . . He helped thousands of people escape from the Nazis during World War Two. Few would suspect that this small, stocky man outsmarted many a killer's effort to purge the Aryan race of "undesirables."

Ms. Kuntz says further: "Father speaks in a low soft voice as if he is afraid the wrong someone will hear him, even while he is in his parish house in serene Mooreton, North Dakota." These words, spoken almost thirty years after the war, epitomize an element in Fr. Paczek's life which will become more evident as the reader goes through this volume: a quiet humble man, a pious man, a man for whom the past was seldom absent. There was a sense of caution, even fear that marked his life. (Among his personal papers at his death there was found a permit to carry a concealed weapon.)

Given his reticence, the portrayal of his life has been difficult. Six different historical archives in Warsaw have been searched, so also a Home Army archive in Torun, Poland. In Poland also, A. Sieriszecka has been of great help. The Pallottine Fathers' archives in Warsaw has been contacted. But they, like other sources in that city, have been working at a real disability. The almost complete destruction of Warsaw took most records away in the fires of 1944 and 1945. The archives of the London Polish Government in Exile (Studium Polski Podziehnej) have been of considerable help in this search, though much of their intelligence records have disappeared. The Vatican archives has informed us that only today are the World War II files being catalogued and made available for scholars. Even the American FBI has been contacted though the Freedom of Information Act; the United States and Polish Armies were allies throughout the Second World War. And, of course, the files of the Diocese of Fargo were available in the reconstruction of Fr. Paczek's life story. From the above sources, bits and pieces of information have emerged and where needed were translated and used in this volume.

One person has to be gratefully singled out: Alice Biewer, librarian at Lidgerwood, a next-door neighbor and a continued support during the last decade of his life. Mrs. Biewer was custodian of his library for some months after Fr. Paczek's death. She preserved his papers and was a major source of information.

The Veterans of the Polish Home Army in the United States and Canada published newsletters *(Biuletyn Informacyjny);* these have been very helpful. The Internet has a surprisingly large amount of information, for example the War Crimes Trials and Jewish ghetto in Warsaw. Above all, several dozen of Fr. Paczek's former parishioners have shared their recollections, so also many of his priest colleagues have provided information. To all the above, we are grateful. The memories of Fr. Paczek's friends have been clouded with time, but some fragments of his rare comments remain. These, when put together with archival sources, give us a chance to complete, in a limited fashion, the story of his life.

We are most appreciative of the help of Dr. Jan Nowok, who twice accompanied us to Lidgerwood to review and select pertinent portions of Fr. Paczek's papers and certain volumes from his library. Dr. Nowok has guided our search through the maze of European archives and translated a considerable number of documents. In a sense this volume should be dedicated to him. Without his insight and inspiration, much of this volume would never have been recorded on a printed page.

Our thanks go also to three patient translators: Dr. Luke Gasiorowski, Magda Mitek, and Richard Zalewski. Not only did they help us with the words and concepts, but also they have been a great source of information concerning Polish culture and history.

We thank those who gave us permission to use photos and printed materials. An attempt has been made to contact the pertinent publishers.

We are grateful especially to Jerry Anderson of the University of Mary for his admirable assistance in the design and production of this volume, and also to Bev Rosenkrans for typing, editing, and gracious advise in bringing this volume to its completion. Michele Delmore has, likewise, been of great help. The University of Mary and its president, Sister Thomas Welder, has been of special assistance in all of our endeavors. Our thanks go to Bishop Samuel Aquilla and the Diocese of Fargo for continued support through every step in the publication process.

This little volume should be of value to Fr. Paczek's former parishioners and to his clerical friends who wondered about the war memories that lurked in the mind of this devout man who was part of their lives. It may also be an inspiration to pessimistic readers who occasionally wonder if the world could "get any worse." This book should remind us all that we live perhaps in the "best of times." The past was often unbelievably cruel.

CHAPTER ONE

Early Life

FR. VALERIAN PACZEK (Walerian in Polish) was born on October 17, 1909, in the Gdansk portion of Poland. This area, however, until 1920 was part of Germany's Ost Prussia and was strongly influenced by German culture. The exact place of birth was Lipinski-Krolewski near Starogard. The location of his birth and early childhood would prove to be providential for knowledge of German ways would be the foundation of his wartime activities, and, indeed, his very survival in many hostile situations. (There were times in his life that when asked the place of his birth he could answer truthfully, "East Prussia.")

The son of Walerian Paczek and Weronika Wojak, he was part of a family of six children: three brothers, Ksawery, Alojyz, and Jozef, plus two sisters, Jozefa and Waleria, who became a nun.

Apparently the first years of his education took place in a school that used the German language. In fact, later it was said he spoke accent-less German.

At a young age, ten years (?), he left home to attend a boarding school. Later in life he would say that his retirement years at his little house in Lidgerwood were the happiest in his life. In effect, it was the only real home he could ever enjoy.

His first graduation ceremony was in 1928 from the Pallottine High School in Wadowice. (This town, by the way, was the birthplace of Pope John Paul II.) From there he went to a Pallottine Seminary in Oltawa, where he majored in philosophy and theology. His courses of study, which he completed on August 5, 1930, were the routine curricula for seminarians in every part of the globe.

Fr. Paczek, however, must have approached the academic life with a special diligence, for he not only immersed himself in the usual Latin and Greek, but acquired some knowledge of French, Italian, and English. (Later in life, in war and civilian times, he would hear confessions in all these languages. He at one time, for example, was pastor of a Lidgerwood's Bohemian parish (St. John Nepomucene) and in nearby Geneseo's Polish parish. There he would preach and counsel in Czech and Polish.

He was, of course, affiliated with the Pallottine religious community (the official title was Society of the Catholic Apostolate). He therefore spent time in the Pallottine novitiate; this was at Suchary, near Nakla. With the completion of this probationary time, he made special promises to follow faithfully the way of life as outlined by the 19th century founder, St. Vincent Pallotti. Years later he published a small book on St. Vincent and his remarkable religious perspectives.

After four more years of education, this time with a more intense study of theology and other priestly sciences, he received the sacrament of Holy Orders on June 17, 1934. The ordination ceremony was performed by Poland's most prominent prelate, Cardinal A. Hlond. Fr. Paczek, through the years, fondly recalled that it was "a beautiful sunny day" in the city of Poznan.

The Pallottine Society did not let the young priest remain idle. After a brief vacation, he was sent for another year of higher education and by 1935 he was at work in a Pallottine school. There he "supervised over six hundred students," taught language, and gave spiritual direction. Fr. Paczek's resume of those days included the phrase he "helped out with masses for two military regiments." (Even as a young priest, there was a connection to the Armed Forces.)

After his stint in the Pallottine School—it lasted five years—he was appointed in 1938 as Assistant Pastor in a parish in Eastern Poland.

Up to this moment his life seems to have been typical of young priests all over the world: school, ordination, pastoral work. Fr. Paczek was perhaps a little more intellectually inclined and he was obviously pious, but nonetheless, he was typical.

There were, however, clouds on the horizon for him and for thousands of similar young priests. They were entering a decade of time in which many thousands of their parishioners would die and hundreds of their priest colleagues would also die or experience unimaginable violence.

Times were changing. The Russian Communist government, with its menacing military force, had already killed millions in its death camps and would kill millions more in its determination to absorb as much of Europe as possible. In Western Europe, Hitler, with his Nazi ambitions, had absorbed Austria and Czechoslovakia, and was casting an evil eye on Polish land. Fr. Paczek says in a brief note in his 50th anniversary booklet, "Everyone was talking about the possibility of war."

When the young Fr. Paczek reported to his parish in eastern Poland he found it was in the town of Korelicze on the Russian border, not far from the Soviet Republic of the Ukraine. The town today, after the changes following the fall of Communism, is now in the nation of Belarus.

Not only did Fr. Paczek do the usual parish pastoral work, he served in his own words, as a kind of "auxiliary chaplain for two regiments of Polish soldiers."

It is here that the story gets foggy; in fact he never discussed in print or in letters anything of the events between 1938 and 1939. He arrived in Eastern Poland in 1938. He arrived in Warsaw December 20, 1939. What happened?

We know the big picture. Hitler and Stalin reached a secret agreement that would allow their respective armies to invade Poland. The Germans would take the western half of the nation (which included Warsaw). The Russians would take the east. Fr. Paczek, with his parishioners and military regiments, would be the first to be overwhelmed.

We might call this period of his life the "silent year," silent in the sense that there is no "paper trail." The reader will have to be patient. Much of the following comes from the casual comments that still remain in the memories of parishioners, friends, and priest companions.

On September 1, 1939, Germany invaded Western Poland. Their highly refined army and air force destroyed the Polish defending forces. Poles fought courageously, but lost their battles and suffered great casualties. On September 17th the Soviet armies crossed the eastern border. Fr. Paczek, in his 50th anniversary booklet, says, quite succinctly: "We were attacked from both sides, we fought knowing that we would be unable to resist."

Indeed the Polish fought. The ensuing events of what became a global war have eclipsed the Polish heroism. (Against the Germans alone, 60,000 Poles were killed; another 135,000 were wounded.) Little attention has been given to the Polish sufferings, for within a matter of days England and France, bound by treaties, declared war on Germany. Events rushed on. Within a year, France was overwhelmed by German forces and England was besieged on its ocean-surrounded island. (Remember, it was a year later, on December 7, 1941, with the Japanese attack on Pearl Harbor, that America went to war with both Germany and Japan.)

The Polish fought desperately in every part of their nation. On the Eastern front they were smothered by the masses of Soviet troops. Some 190,000 Polish captured enlisted men were summarily loaded on trains and taken to slave labor (gulag) camps. Fifteen thousand officers were swept up and sent to special camps in the Russian interior. The Russians were determined to eliminate the Polish presence in the eastern portion of their occupied zone. In all, a half million Poles, soldiers and civilians, disappeared into Russian captivity. These were Fr. Paczek's parishioners! They not only went to the Russian camps, most never returned.

It was during these times that Stalin ordered the execution of Polish officers. As history shows, 4,321 were shot and buried in mass graves at Katyn in 1943. A large proportion of the 15,000 were likewise executed at places like Kalinin and Kharkov in the Ukraine.

Father Paczek was, as chaplain, involved in the fighting. Among his papers there was found a "Diplom" of 1980; with that document was a notation that he had received a gold medal. It was from the Association of "Soldiers of Eastern Polish Areas." (Clearly he had been active as a soldier-chaplain on the Polish Eastern Front.)

Yet Fr. Paczek never wrote about this fateful part of his life. From comments gathered, however, he must have been on the trains taking the officers to the Russian Gulag camps. Several North Dakota friends mention this story: the train was heading east and it slowed down on a wooded hill. With a companion, Fr. Paczek jumped from the train and ran desperately for hours and finally escaped. One story remembers him saying he was lying in the brush and heard the sound of soldiers' boots near his head, as they were searching for escapees. On another occasion, Fr. Paczek told of lying, half covered with debris, with dirt in his eyes and on his face. Russian soldiers were moving through the group of bodies, shooting those who seemed to be alive. Another person remembers him saying he hid, frightened, in a culvert to avoid capture.

Not all the Polish soldiers allowed themselves to be sent to Russia. Many ran from capture, heading for Hungary and Rumania. (These countries were still neutral.) In fact, we know now that at that very time, over seventy thousand Poles were crossing the southern Carpathian Mountains, seeking by any means to get to the free Western world. Many were determined to continue the war in Allied armies. In England alone, several thousand Polish airmen eventually arrived to be part of the Royal Air Force. (In the famous 1940 Battle of Britain, Polish units were among the most accomplished and most decorated of all the air contingents.)

The records show Fr. Paczek arrived in Warsaw December 20, 1939. The Russian invasions began September 17th of that year. For him that four-month period would inevitably contain some moments of high drama.

Perhaps he was part of the stream of Polish patriots who surged through the mountains on their way to freedom. If he took the Balkan route he was well equipped to do so for he had a fluency in languages. He could have managed very well with his knowledge of Slavic, Germanic, and Latin-based languages. He could have followed the trails and roads using guides who worked for money or because of hatred for Germans and Russians.

There are reports that in his struggle to evade the Russians he was captured a second time and again escaped. (Perhaps this was the "lying-in-debris" occasion.) He mentioned to a priest friend that he had an automatic pistol with 12 cartridges. He was determined, he said, that if he were caught a third time, he would "take twelve Russians with him." (He was an excellent marksman. A parishioner at Lidgerwood saw him doing practice with blackbirds as targets.)

If he took the Balkan route, he must have "doubled back" to enter the German-occupied portion of Poland and then made his way to Warsaw. There's no denying it, getting through the German border outposts must have been a scary enterprise.

Fr. Paczek's struggle to reach Warsaw could have involved a more direct route, one which from our half-century-later perspective seems to have been nearly impossible. He could have crossed, by dodging and hiding, through the Russian lines, through the "no man's land," and finally through the German border outpost-obstructions and then traveled to Warsaw.

A passing comment to a North Dakota friend years later seems to corroborate the second hypothesis. He spoke of a time when he crossed Russian lines with the help of a "local" farm family. Yet he never elaborated on the time and location.

Years later, he attributed his escapes from the grasp of the Russians to the "help of the Blessed Mother." With such help, we can certainly agree that the "impossible" could be accomplished. Late in life he would write that there were "six times" in which his life was saved through the protection of the Virgin Mary. As the reader proceeds in this volume, some of these six incidents will become evident.

Sources in print say that on December 20, 1939, Fr. Paczek came to Warsaw. The approximately four months between that date and the Russian invasion, September 4th, make up his silent days. As seen above, we have only hearsay and conjectures to fill in the empty spaces.

CHAPTER TWO

In Warsaw

ARRIVING IN WARSAW the end of December, Fr. Paczek saw a capital already filled with war damage. German divisions on the rush through Poland had encircled the city. Ninety thousand Polish troops were defending its parameters. The Germans subjected the city to fierce artillery and air bombardment. The city had been famous as a place of beauty, with grand churches, ancient palaces, charming streets of stone, and half-timbered buildings. When Fr. Paczek saw it, rubble and scars of war could be seen on every side.

The German propagandists' attitudes toward Poles during the war was frightening. Hitler had authorized some of his units, where needed, "to kill without mercy, men, women, and children of Polish origin." The official Nazi philosophy saw Poles and Eastern Europeans as "subhumans," only one step above Jews.

With the end of hostilities, some western and central parts of Poland were annexed directly into Germany. Poles were to be cast out of these areas. Polish schools and many churches were shut down. Museums and theaters were closed. The rest of Poland was placed under a German governor, Hans Frank, a fanatical Nazi, who saw Poland as "a gigantic labor camp." Radios were forbidden, car ownership was curtailed, and permits were needed to travel. Almost from the beginning of the German occupation, executions took place and thousands of citizens were being scooped up and sent to labor and concentration camps.

Warsaw, fortunately, was not in the annexed territory but many of the same restrictions were in place. It was a reign of terror, which gradually spread over the city and the land.

The average Pole was seething within. Polish national loyalty was not a new thing. Poles were aware of the wars and invasions of the past. The Polish National Anthem began with this phrase: "Poland Is Not Yet Dead." It is not surprising that the Polish government, unwilling to submit to another occupying force, transferred itself, in the last days of hostilities, to London and from there continued to direct as well as it could the affairs of Polish people at home and abroad. It took the name of the Polish Government in Exile or the Free Polish Government. General W. Sikorski became the president and he was surrounded by a variety of department heads, one of which had to do with what became known as the Polish Home Army, the A.K. These were the underground forces in the homeland.

The influence of the London Free Government was not imaginary; it directed tens of thousands of Polish soldiers, many who escaped through the Balkan countries. They were now part of the 2nd Polish Army Corps, fighting eventually in the Mid East, Africa, and some of their comrades were later involved in the invasions of Italy, France and the Low Lands. These were augmented by thousands of Polish soldiers, former prisoners, who were released from Russian camps to travel by way of Iran to British North Africa.

The Polish Home Army, the Armia Krajowa, came into existence almost the very day of the Polish capitulation to the Germans. Men and women in every part of the country were eventually involved. By the end of the German occupation, they numbered at least 400,000 members. Post-war scholars say no country had an underground that was so extensive.

The Home Army had as its nucleus 11,000 former Polish Army officers; an equal number of civilians were eventually trained to take up leadership positions. Arms such as rifles, machine guns, grenades, and even some artillery pieces were hidden throughout Poland. Some of the equipment and ammunition was left over from the Polish Army deposits; some was stolen from the Germans, and some came by way of air drops from England. It was all controlled by the Free Government in England, but more immediately by a remarkable underground leader,

General Tadeusz Bor-Komorowski (always known by his pseudonym, "Bor"). The AK or Home Army had its regular departments: intelligence, operations, supply, tribunal, communication, and information. (It published a number of limited edition newspapers.)

It was into this war-damaged but secretly mobilizing Warsaw that Fr. Paczek entered at the end of December 1939. As a good cleric, he reported to his superiors at the Pallottine House near the Old Town part of the city. Fr. Paczek wrote years later to a Polish scholar: "I lived at Dluga 15 [street number] which was the Pallottine residence; the former palace of Bishop Gawlina." This three-story house was next to the Garnizonowy Church. (Both the church and Bishop Gawlina will be part of this story as it unfolds in the following pages.)

Fr. Paczek immediately took an assignment as chaplain to the adjacent Red Cross Hospital (an institution with the same name but no association with the International Red Cross organization). His task, as one would expect, was to care for the spiritual needs of the sick and the dying. The hospital was a prestigious institution, with medical students, nursing students, and a highly acclaimed staff. The staff, as well as the patients, became Fr. Paczek's concern; he offered Mass each day and gave sermons and retreats.

Yet with all his responsibilities, Fr. Paczek was still able to pursue his intellectual goals. The Germans had already thrown various Polish professors into concentration camps. In Krakow, the famed Jagiellonian University, had been shut down. In that city, Karol Wojtyla, the future pope, was taking courses from Krakow university professors in underground classrooms. In Warsaw, enough scholars were present to set up a kind of clandestine University of Warsaw faculty, offering courses with a minimum of fanfare. Fr. Paczek began the pursuit of a Master's in Church Law. One of his professors said to him, "In times like this, in such a situation, to survive, one must have two wings, knowledge and faith." In spite of the almost complete destruction of the city in 1944-45, some school records managed to survive. The Catholic Theological Academy in 1958 issued this certificate: "The Reverend Walerian Paczek received a Master's Degree in Canon Law on June 22, 1945." Apparently after peace was restored, Fr. Paczek, by then a Major in a displaced persons camp in Germany, formally received his long-desired degree.

Almost from his first days in Warsaw, Fr. Paczek realized he could not ignore the ferment around him. At his place of residence, the Pallottine house at 15 Dluga Street, there resided a remarkable individual, Fr. Franciszek Paulinski, both the house superior and a teacher of classical languages. This man was already in contact with the underground movement. With the consent, even the encouragement of Fr. Paulinski, Fr. Paczek and the other young Pallottine priests offered their assistance to the Home Army. Ringing in their ears were the warnings of their superior: "Be discreet in your activities, be sensitive to danger, be cautious in all conversations, and reveal nothing of your work." If there was ever a deviation from these principles, they would be banished from Dluga 15.

Soon Fr. Paczek was introduced to Fr. Tadeusz Jachimowski, the chief of the underground priests. At the same time he met Fr. Jachimowski's deputy, Fr. Tadeusz Sienkiewicz. Fr. Paczek was designated as liaison priest in contact with the underground in the Zoliborz part of the city and with other sectors, where needed. (In the 1944 Uprising his tasks took him more and more to Zoliborz, but often back to the Old Town area.)

The decision to make him a liaison priest was probably because his chaplaincy at the Red Cross Hospital provided him with documents which enabled him to move at odd hours through the city; he would be "attending the sick." Certainly it was a tribute to his fluency in German and his childhood origins in "East Prussia." A post war tribute added the following reason for his choice: "His own personal qualities, and his internal discipline."

Everyone involved in key underground functions was given a pseudonym (a false name). All communications and documents used these code names. There was the constant concern for Gestapo infiltration and their ability to "roll up" the various Home Army units.

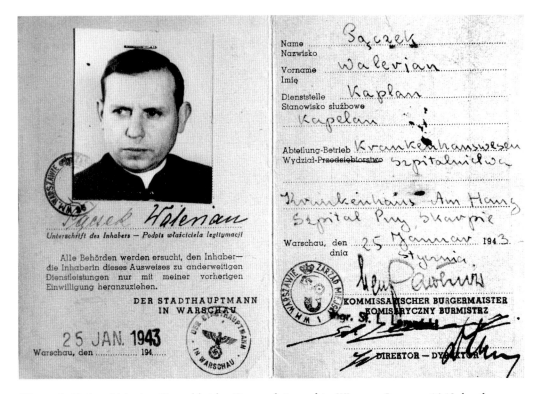

Figure 1. Father Valerian Paczek's identity card, issued in Warsaw, January 1943, by the occupying Germans. Reissued twice a year, it lists his occupation as chaplain.

Fr. Paczek's code name was "Germen." The name became so important and so personal that even decades after the war, in correspondence, his friends often referred to each other as "Rog," "Alfons," and like names. In fact, Fr. Paczek's own printed discussion of the war carefully lists the code as well as the personal names of his military associates.

The name "Germen" was chosen, according to author Jan Dobraczynski, because of his knowledge of the German language. But also it had its roots in the

Latin word "Germen," which means a "bud" or something from which life arises (see the English word "germinated").

The duties of "Germen" involved not only carrying messages from one unit to another, it also meant listening to free world radio programs (probably from Britain) and disseminating this information to underground officials, particularly the underground press. Warsaw had 150 secret printing machines in basements throughout the city which turned out posters, flyers, newspapers, and at times counterfeit credentials. Indeed, one of Fr. Paczek's jobs was to carry printed materials to Home Army units, and even to church authorities.

The Red Cross Hospital to which he was attached was highly regarded and German officers, when ill, rather than go to the often-temporary German field facilities, would prefer physicians in an up-to-date "regular" institution. Fr. Paczek (and other medical staff who spoke German) would "innocently" overhear conversations. This information, if of value, would go to an underground intelligence unit and would often be sent to London by radio, or perhaps even by courier.

Warsaw's harsh days and months stretched into years. Fr. Paczek lived in these tense times, from 1940 to the middle of 1944. In a tribute to Fr. Paczek, published in an American Home Army Veterans *Biuletyn,* the writer, in Polish, said, "It was a period that was exceptional, a time in which many people lapsed into doubt, many broke mentally and thought only of saving their own personal life. Yet this same dramatic period unlocked for some individuals great internal power. The priest we honor mobilized his strength and doubled his efforts for his faith and his homeland."

The German Gestapo was ever alert. Some Poles became collaborators. A slip of the tongue could bring a series of arrests. Capture by the Germans would mean torture, sometimes a Nazi concentration camp, and probably death. A post-war estimate said 185 Polish priests, from different parts of the country, "lost their lives for their participation in 'illegal' activities." The report continued, "Germans were always searching for these men." If this was the case among priests, how many Polish laymen and women were swept up in Gestapo raids and sent to their deaths?

One of the secrets of his endurance and commitment to his country was Fr. Paczek's spiritual life. He stated this very clearly in a note attached to a brief resume of his life. "Considering the Polish situation, I stopped into the Capuchin Church (Kosciol O. O. Kapucynow) and kneeling in front of the picture of the Mother of God, made an oath. Let it be your will, if I go through this storm [sic] successfully, I will be praying three parts of the rosary each day until the end of my life." (Apparently in Polish, a "part" of a rosary is a decade; nonetheless a parishioner 30 years later, in North Dakota, remembers joining him at times as he recited three rosaries in one prayer session.)

One of Fr. Paczek's tasks was to carry what his comrades later recorded as "very large" or "huge" sums of money. He was to deliver these funds to various underground units. He once wrote that on one occasion while carrying money he noticed, ahead of him, the Germans were making a "round-up sweep near the railroad station." He said, "I told the street car driver to move the car slowly through the German soldiers without stopping. We succeeded!" When he reached a safe area he got to a phone and warned others of the police action.

How many close calls he must have had: we can only guess. Years later Fr. Paczek recalled another hair-raising event:

> I was on a street car when German soldiers stopped it near the Church of St. Cross. I was on my way to the hospital about six o'clock in the morning, and I had a large sum of money in my briefcase. I was frightened. Two German officers noticed it and asked me to get out of the street car to check my I.D. One of them began searching my briefcase. In one pocket of my briefcase he found a Bible and in the second pocket some hard bread. He looked at this and asked, "what is this?" "This is my meal," I responded. "I'll consume it, I have to work hard, likely to 5 o'clock P.M." The officer thought for a while and let me go. Thanks to God I thought, in the third pocket I had the money.

Moments like this were engraved in Fr. Paczek's memory. In his elderly years he would speak of the six times he was saved by divine intervention. This episode with the German officer surely must have been one of the six.

The mention of huge sums of money brings up the question of its origin. Where did it come from? The answer is, of course, from England, from the Polish Free Government and from Allied government allotments. Records show as much. *The Secret History of the SOE* (English Special Operations) says in June 1941, 600,000 pounds were designated for subversive work in continental Europe. The American OSS (underground operations) was also channeling money to occupied countries. In 1944-45, for example, it had 25 million dollars to use for such purposes.

How did the money get from London to Poland? Did it involve Fr. Paczek? Here again printed records do not help us. The 1977 interview in *Fare Three Well* concerning Fr. Paczek says this: "He (Fr. Paczek) emphasizes there are many things he will not reveal about his life because of his concern that certain information about his undercover activities during and after the war could still endanger either himself or someone else in the Communist world."

Bits of conversations, still in the memories of his former parishioners and priest friends, say Fr. Paczek, as a courier, did go to England during his Warsaw years. The border with Yugoslavia and Rumania was porous, that we know. As mentioned previously, though certain areas were occupied by Germans, a series of local guides could and did take people through the mountains and trails. Partisan forces abounded in these lands. Certainly a German and Slavic-speaking individual, with a knowledge of Latin-based languages, would be ideal for such an undertaking.

Friends heard Fr. Paczek mention frequently dodging German patrols, crossing waters by boat, even visiting the Vatican in the wartime days. In fact, he was said to have been bringing communications from Polish bishops to the Vatican Secretary of State, Monsignor Montini. On his return trip to Poland, he carried messages back to the Polish hierarchy. He was, accordingly, working for two masters: the Polish-British forces and the Catholic authorities.

Figure 2. Father Valerian
Paczek during a visit with
Pope John Paul II, in 1984.

Fr. Paczek could never return to Poland, as will be seen later in this volume, and he felt he was in danger well after the war. He did on two occasions take groups of pilgrims from the North Dakota to Rome. In 1984 he was given a private audience with the Pope. And it was true that Pope John Paul II knew of his wartime activities. The Pope had been Bishop of Krakow and priests who had been in the underground or the camps would certainly have told him of Fr. Paczek, or "Germen," as he was known. Yet when he was in Rome he told his friends, "Don't mention in public that I am here." Why the fear? (Incidentally, the Vatican archives for World War II are just now (2004) being opened. Bishop Samuel Aquila of the Fargo Diocese promises to pursue the search for the Walerian Paczek file. When that happens some interesting material may be forthcoming.)

Yet, when Fr. Paczek went into the Vatican "inner quarters" to see the Pope, the Vatican guards saluted with honor, addressing him as "Father Colonel Paczek."

(An American bishop hoped to go in with him, but the guards said, "I'm sorry, Your Excellency. This is just for Fr. Colonel Paczek.")

An occasional story concerning Fr. Paczek and the war mentions his somehow getting to Spain, a neutral country, and then traveling to London. An Irish-born priest friend remembered Fr. Paczek joking about "the red carpet treatment" he recieved when he arrived in London. The British authorities provided him with a personal car and driver while in the city and awaiting a parachute drop back into Poland. All this activity would take place ostensibly during what Fr. Paczek would tell his authorities was, "a vacation from his hospital tasks."

There were occasions in which Fr. Paczek would talk about dropping by parachute, aiming at pinpoints of light on the ground. Home Army members would use lanterns or torches to outline a drop area. (It could be that others would drop with him. British sources recorded 340 "drops" to Occupied Poland—one estimate says there were 485 drops.) All this had to be done by multi-engine aircraft, for it was at least 700 miles from England to Warsaw. The journey was often over Denmark and Sweden. Such events, to say the least, were suspenseful. Fr. Paczek mentioned having a cyanide capsule in his jaw during the descent. If Germans held the lights, instant suicide would be an option. Few individuals were able to stand up under Gestapo torture; information obtained could unmask a whole series of underground operatives. The matter of a cyanide capsule for suicide brings up, for a Catholic, a real moral question: "The end does not justify the means." But, after all, this was wartime. We have to let the ethicists argue the question. And we will never know whether Fr. Paczek would have ever resorted to using the "emergency" device.

Was Fr. Paczek imagining things? Did he actually drop by air from England? Was he talking about friends who had done courier service to London? To be honest, this writer feels the story is true. Too many of his war episodes have seemed to be almost impossible, but when archival materials have arrived from Polish or English language sources, what appeared to be hearsay proved to be true. But even more, the story of dropping in the night, praying that he might land among friends, was heard by a number of astute North Dakota listeners. There had to be a substance of truth to it.

Warsaw, in the days of German occupation, was a frightful place. The sounds and smells of evil were everywhere present; there was the frequent tramp of German boots, the sound of German tanks. German guards were in the streets and historic landmark buildings were filled with the uniforms of the despised *"Niemcy"* (Germans). Certain areas were marked "For Germans Only." Regularly whispers floated around concerning friends who were arrested and disappeared. At night, neighborhoods would hear vans pulling up to doorways, the shouts of the Gestapo, and the protests of loved ones being hauled away to unknown places.

All the while there were reports from secret radios about battles taking place in Russia, North Africa, Italy, and Greece. The Warsaw civilians were well aware that Polish military units, often under their own General W. Anders, were involved in those "free world" contests. They knew, too, that thousands of Polish men, as aviators and sailors, fought in Britain's Royal Air Force and alongside the British Navy. Hope was in the atmosphere, but how long would it take to realize freedom?

Figure 3. The symbol of the Polish Underground Home Army (AK). "P" and "W" means "Poland fights." The anchor is a sign of hope.

The underground army had its symbol: a cross and anchor combination, combining the letters "W" and "P." ("Fighting Poland," it meant; the anchor was the ancient symbol for hope.) This "logo" was scrawled on walls a thousand times throughout Poland as a reminder to all, friend or foe, of the presence of the underground. Not that the Germans needed to be reminded, for the Home Army regularly blew up trains, attacked Gestapo headquarters, and assassinated German officials. In response, the occupiers retaliated with special viciousness, killing individuals and sometimes whole groups of civilians. All this was part of the daily perceptions of Warsaw residents.

Most frightening of all, perhaps, were the decisions by the occupying forces, starting in 1940, to place Warsaw's Jews in a walled-off ghetto. And there were many Jews; almost ten percent of Poland before the war was of Jewish background. The ghetto was a fifty regular and odd-sized block area, only a five-minute walk from Dluga 15. The establishment of the ghetto in 1940 was just the beginning of the Nazi's effort to eliminate Poland's Jews. In May 1942, the first contingent of Jews reached the Auschwitz-Birkenau camp. An estimated 1,500,000 were said to have been eventually exterminated at that location. (It must be mentioned that with them were 50,000 Christian Poles.)

In all, over 400,000 Jews were initially within the walls of the Warsaw ghetto. They lived in appalling conditions with marginal food supplies and minimal health and sanitary facilities. (By the end of 1943, 300,000 had died from transport to death camps or execution.) Some Warsaw residents tried to "look elsewhere," ignoring as much as possible the plight of their Jewish countrymen. A post-war historian wrote: "The Nazis promulgated a law in Poland unique in all of occupied Europe; it formally established that any Pole helping a Jew would automatically receive the death penalty . . . a Pole who gave as much as a glass of water to a Jew outside of the ghetto was liable to be shot. A Pole who failed to report to the authorities knowledge of a Jew in hiding was unfailingly deported to a concentration camp."

On the other hand, many Warsaw non-Jews, in spite of the death threat, were attempting to provide help. One historian calculated that as many as 80,000 Christian Poles helped Jews during the four years of Warsaw persecution. There was a secret organization put together just for the purpose of providing aid to Warsaw's Jews; it took the name *Zegota.* Its objective was to get any aid possible to the ghetto residents, to help Jews escape and even to get money and arms into the walled-off area. Communication was done in a variety of ways, but the Warsaw sewer system and tunnels were used extensively.

Fr. Paczek was active in these endeavors, this is very clear. In a letter to the *Los Angeles Times* (February 19, 1982), a Polish Home Army veteran challenged a columnist's assertion that few Poles were involved in helping Warsaw's Jews. The writer, Tadeusz Borowski, said the following: "Here, residing in the USA, there is another survivor of the events, Rev. Dr. Valerian Paczek, Lt. Col. Ret., Chief Chaplain of the Home Army Warsaw region serving from 1939 till 1944. He personally took part in the action called 'Zegota,' planned and executed with the only purpose to support the Jewish front with all means available."

The Zegota operation had regular communication with the ghetto, the sewers, of course, but also through disguised workmen, occasional breaks in the walls, and through tunnels. Arms, money, and information were passed to the beleaguered Jews. Historian Richard Lukas says in *Forgotten Holocaust* that Zegota forged, in two years, 50,000 documents for Jews. It is now well recognized that Zegota not only assisted adult Jews to escape, but they succeeded in smuggling 2,500 Jewish children from the ghetto. These young people were placed in Christian homes and given new names. (Their real identities were recorded, placed in jars and often buried so that reunions with families might be possible after the war.)

Efforts to save Jews took place all over Poland. The Zegota efforts have in recent years received a considerable amount of attention. A post-war book by a Jewish scholar, Nechama Tec, *When Light Pierced the Darkness,* details some of the story. Often the assistance was on a person-to-person level, but sometimes it was an organized effort. The book was published in 1986 by New York's Oxford University Press.

One evening a distinguished physician, a surgeon on the Red Cross hospital staff, came to Fr. Paczek with a dilemma. He said he had received a call from the ghetto. There was a very sick woman who needed an operation that was so complicated the Jewish doctors couldn't handle it. The doctor said he could do it, "but if I go, I may be shot. What should I do?" Fr. Paczek replied that in justice his duty was first toward his patients in the hospital, but in charity, love of his fellow humans, that was a different matter; "You will have to decide." The physician, Dr. Franciszek Raszeja, thought for a while and then said he would go to the ghetto. He first went to confession, received a blessing, collected his equipment and departed. While performing the operation the Gestapo burst in and shot both the patient and the physician. Fr. Paczek said that within a few hours after his departure, Dr. Raszeja's body was brought back to the hospital, pierced with bullets.

Holy Cross Hospital was destroyed in the 1944 hostilities. But a new, equally prestigious hospital exists today in Poznan, Poland, bearing the name Franciszek Raszeja. It stands as a symbol of German brutality and Polish concern for Jews.

Father Paczek ("Germen") was deeply involved in aid to the Warsaw Jews. A carbon copy of a letter exists, sent to a Polish officer-scholar (dated October 14, 1966), in which he writes, "I gave shelter to five Jewish families" and "I was giving out certificates of birth to whole Jewish families with names of persons who had died sometime before in the hospital."

Fr. Paczek was not single-handed in this false identification project. Jews throughout Poland changed their identity and became "Gentile" through documents prepared by Catholic clergy. Certainly other Warsaw colleagues of Fr. Paczek were involved. Though he mentions birth certificates, this was only part of a parcel of documents obtained from many Catholic parish files. The baptism and confirmation, even marriage records of the deceased Catholic would be gathered and distributed. But that was not all. Clandestine classes in some parts of Poland would be held in which the escaped person would memorize Catholic prayers and become acquainted with elementary Catholic doctrines and rituals. Suspicious Gestapo police would, at times, grill the individual to ascertain the veracity of their "Catholic" status.

Post-war Polish accounts speak of a dozen Catholic institutions which helped "rescue" Warsaw's Jews. Within walking distance of Fr. Paczek's home there were the Church of All Saints at Grzybowski Square, the Church of the Nativity on Leszno Street, and the Church of the Holy Virgin. Also aiding Jews were personnel at St. John's Cathedral and St. Augustine's Church. Nearby convents were involved, like the

Carmelites and the nuns at the Resurrection House. So Fr. Paczek's work was being carried out throughout the city, but especially in the downtown-Old Town area.

Fr. Paczek's reference to saving five Jewish families in his house is accurate. The top floor of the Pallottine residence at Dluga 15, up under the eaves, was the place of hiding. Fr. Paczek, of course, had associates in this particular rescue project; other Pallottine priests were involved. Most notable would be their superior, Fr. Paulinski. This gentleman is mentioned in several sources as a key figure in Pallottine secret work.

The interview with LuAnn Kuntz in the North Dakota booklet *Fare Thee Well* gives further details: the papers "Germen" helped manufacture assisted Jews not only to escape Warsaw, but to get over the borders to another country (Hungary and Rumania were under German rule only in the last period of World War II.)

The central role of Fr. Paczek in these activities is corroborated by the recollection of three different North Dakota friends who, on separate occasions, heard him recount this story: One time he was on an airplane from Chicago to Minneapolis. He sat next to a gentleman and began a casual conversation. Soon it became apparent that both men were from Poland. The companion ventured the fact that he was "Jewish." Fr. Paczek asked him how he "got out." The gentleman said, in effect, he took on a new Christian identity. To prove it the man took from his wallet a copy of a Christian birth and baptismal certificate (one, no doubt, he kept to show his Catholic friends). Fr. Paczek studied the document closely and then asked to use the man's pen. He wrote on a separate piece of paper much of the information (one account said he used his left hand) and it became apparent that this was a document that Fr. Paczek himself had "manufactured." Needless to say, the man was excited and wanted "the good Father" to visit him and meet his family. Fr. Paczek had to decline. He said he must return to his parish for scheduled masses.

A final note: A search has been made of the archives of the Jewish historical offices in Warsaw (Zydowski Instytut Historyzny). Nothing concerning Fr. Paczek could be found. This is not surprising for Germans destroyed 85 to 90 percent of the city after the Uprising. Likewise, the records of the Pallottine headquarters at Dluga 15 and Miodowa 16 we now know were "destroyed by fire."

In Israel there exists today an institution entitled Vad Vashen. Herein is contained a memorial dedicated to the "Righteous" who saved Jews during the years of persecution. As of 1984, 5,742 heroic individuals were on the honor list and 1,505 were of Polish background. Fr. Paczek's name is not on the list. When asked about the number, the Director, Dr. Palpiel, estimated that to obtain a real number of the "Righteous," one would have to multiply that 5,742 number by ten . . . most Jews were helped by a number of individuals, many went by pseudonyms, some were just unnamed faces, and some of their rescuers preferred anonymity.

The Jewish ghetto, originally about 50 blocks, was slowly contracting in size, as more and more Jews were executed or sent to death camps. (By 1943 it was 30-block area.) This wretched place, surrounded by its walls, was ever on the minds of the people at Dluga 15. Already in 1941, a German edict said any Jews leaving the ghetto would be "shot to death" and indeed, executions regularly took place. Accordingly, the sounds of gunfire and the roar of prisoner trucks were often in the ears of Fr. Paczek and his underground friends. The book *When Light Pierced the Darkness* said, "With time the search for escaping Jews and their Polish resources was stepped up and the terror became greater and greater." For many Warsaw Poles it was only with great pain that they heard of the events in the ghetto. There was word that the Jewish police in the ghetto had to turn over to German execution squads a daily quota of Jews who were ultimately to be exterminated. If the quotas were not met, they themselves would be executed. (By summer of 1942, the quota sometimes reached 10,000 per day.) As March 1943 ended, the population of the ghetto had declined from 400,000 to 35,000.

By mid-April, 1943, the Germans began the final liquidation of the Warsaw ghetto. It was at that time when an approximate 1,500 Jewish fighters began a desperate rebellion. They had their own secret stores of weapons, some of which had been smuggled to them by the Home Army. (The London Polish Free Government tried to alert the world to the atrocities. On May 5th it broadcast: "The greatest crime in history is being committed.") The ensuing battle was a lopsided affair, a relative handful of Jewish men against thousands of German assault troops. The fighting continued until May 16. Building by building, the area was razed. The ghetto was a huge sea of fire. All the ghetto occupants were sent to death camps or executed on the spot. Yet a few managed to escape through the tunnels and sewers, with the aid of Polish underground members.

For all Warsaw residents, the tragic fate of the Jews must have been a forewarning of what could happen to them. German racial policy before the war had decreed, "both Poles and Jews are to be kept at an equally low standard of living, and deprived of all rights, both political and national." Hitler himself had said about the young members of his "Master Race," "I want a youth capable of violence, masterful, inflexible, cruel."

But there was hope. Hidden radios and the underground press spread an array of regular reports on happenings on battlefronts. By spring 1944, they knew the Allies had already forced the Germans out of Africa and were in the lower portions of Italy. They knew also that the Soviet armies had re-conquered most of Belarus, the Ukraine, and some of the Baltic Territory. In fact, the Russians were rapidly approaching Poland itself. Certainly they could sense the increased nervousness of the rank and file German troops in their midst. By June 1944 the Polish public knew that American and British forces had invaded Normandy and that Free Polish soldiers were with them in the struggle.

Deep in the Polish soul was a sense of anger over their defeat by German armies in 1939. The Home Army spread throughout the country, by mid-1944 numbering hundreds of thousands of men and women and requiring as many as 25 German divisions to assert their "control." It was the largest underground army in Europe. All these hidden Polish "soldiers" were obsessed with the idea of liberation. Part of their determination was that they themselves wanted at least to help in freeing their country from the heel of the Nazi tyrants. They didn't want history to say that the Russians, or even the Allies, liberated their country while they sat passively to the side.

For four years the Poles had been preparing for the great liberation moment. They had accumulated a mass of arms and, we now know that the Home Army had destroyed, by the end of summer 1944, 6,900 railway engines, and 19,000 railcars. They had also destroyed by hit-and-run operations almost 40 bridges. Six thousand German soldiers and officials had been killed (among them were 2,000 Gestapo agents). An estimated 5,000 aviation engines proved defective, along with 93,000 artillery shells; Polish conscripted laborers were making sure these items would malfunction. The scene, therefore, was set for an uprising.

Tensions were rising. Fr. Tadeusz Jachimowski, Chief Chaplain of all underground clergy, ordered Fr. Paczek to tell his North Group chaplains (at least a dozen in number) to get their emergency religious supplies ready for action.

By the end of July 1944, the word went out that the Soviets had broken German lines east of Warsaw and would soon come to the Vistula River on the edge of the city itself. This prompted the Home Army Commander, General Bor Komorowski, with the approval of the Free Polish Government in London, to set the time for a general revolt. It was to be at 5 p.m. on August 1, 1944.

CHAPTER THREE

Uprising

FR. PACZEK WAS AWARE of the pending uprising. The exact time and the full details were, for him, somewhat vague; he was, after all, a chaplain, not a field officer. When the fateful day arrived, August 1, he seemed to have been taken by surprise. In a 1966 letter to Jan Dobraczynski, he said he was in the student part of Warsaw and wanted to get back to his quarters on Dluga Street, near the Old Town. He couldn't do so. "The students started shooting before the deadline." One historian said, "Although the Germans knew about preparations for the uprising, nevertheless some motorized columns, marching troops, and individual soldiers were surprised by the insurgents, and soon the streets of the capital were strewn with their bodies. . . . At nightfall, elated inhabitants swarmed into the streets and crisscrossed them with a network of barricades."

Concerning the next day, August 2nd, Fr. Paczek remembered: "On my way in the morning along Dluga Street, close to the Gdansk railroad station, tanks were destroying houses. There was shooting and soldiers were trying to divert passersby." He said one soldier tried to stop him. Fr. Paczek appealed to a harassed young German captain and showed him his credentials. The officer, at first, cursed at him. Fr. Paczek said he would pray for him. The officer calmed down, said "Thank you, Father," and let him go on his way. Fr. Paczek got to his residence and then to the hospital, where "wounded were already coming in."

At about this time he contacted his military commander. The Home Army, it seems, had found it necessary to divide the town into various military areas; among

Figure 4. Civilians building barricades in the streets of Warsaw. Source: Dni Powstania

them were North Group, the Downtown Group, and the South Group. The senior military chaplain, Fr. Stefan Kowalski (code name "Biblia") asked him, "Do you have any reservations? Any hesitation?" Fr. Paczek said, "I just want to serve as a chaplain with fighting units." With that, he was assigned to the North Group, situated in Warsaw's central area. Major Stanislaw Blaszczak ("Rog") was to be his immediate superior, along with Colonel Karol Ziemski ("Wachonowski"), who was soon to command the entire North Group. (Note: Major [later Colonel] Blaszczak and Colonel [later General] Ziemski survived the war. They frequently corresponded with Fr. Paczek, and even met for one or two special reunions.)

During these hectic first days, Fr. Paczek was walking to the Red Cross Hospital and at a corner met the hospital director, who said there was no point in going there, for they had already arrested the hospital personnel. He said "Go to Miodowa 16," nearby. It was a Pallottine house, which was transformed into a hospital and was feeding the hungry. The director said, "Stay there and take care of the wounded."

(The Red Cross Hospital would soon be reopened. Fr. Paczek's hospital chaplaincy continued there for at least a few more days.)

On August 7th, Colonel Ziemski ("Wachonowski") appointed Fr. Paczek Dean (Chief Chaplain) of the clergy attached to the North Group. Archives still contain the yellowed order, signed by "Biblia," appointing "Germen" to that position.*

During the first few days of the fighting, Fr. Paczek was about to cross the street after visiting the hospital. There he met Bishop Adamski, a member of the hierarchy who stayed close to the Uprising events. The Bishop stopped him and wanted to be "briefed" on news at home and abroad, for he knew Fr. Paczek was listening to foreign radio broadcasts. While they were talking, shells landed in the street at the very spot where Fr. Paczek would have been walking. After picking themselves up and catching their breath, the Bishop said, "See, Walerian, I saved your life." Fr. Paczek wrote later, "Indeed he did. I would have been at that very place." Bishop Adamski asked for some personal prescriptions and Fr. Paczek took him to a lady-physician who checked his health and gave him medicines that were appropriate.

Fighting intensified and Fr. Paczek moved back and forth from the various medical facilities and into battle areas. Wounded, both Polish and German soldiers were coming into emergency wards. In a brief post-war reminiscence, "Germen" said one time he noticed several severely wounded German soldiers. "Since I spoke German, I heard the confession of one soldier and gave him the sacraments. One of the Germans pleaded with me to ask the doctors not to kill him. I answered, 'Everything will be all right. These doctors are Catholic and not gangsters.' The soldier said, 'Thank you. I see things now in a different light.'"

A ferocious set of battles gradually developed. Not only did they focus on the downtown areas, but elsewhere in the city where there were bastions of fighters;

* Years after the war, Fr. Henryk Szklarek wrote that he, not "Germen" was appointed the North Group's chief chaplain. There was a bit of controversy, but it seems that Fr. Szklarek was to be appointed, but he was absent (wounds ?) and Col. Ziemski appointed Fr. Paczek to that position. In 1965, Colonel Ziemski wrote in a well-publicized letter, that Fr. Paczek, was, indeed, the chief chaplain.

Figure 5. The sewers beneath the streets the streets of Warsaw were important lines of communication during the uprising. Source: Powstanie Warszawskie

not far away was the Zoliborz section, so also Wola, Ochota, and Mokotow. In retrospect, military historians say the Home Army made mistakes; they spread their forces instead of unifying their efforts. But even in downtown Warsaw, the North Group often had to communicate with units a few blocks away through underground passageways.

Each group had its commanders, its fighters, and its chaplains. Fr. Paczek, "Germen," writes in his Fiftieth Anniversary Booklet, "Our duties as chaplains were to perform priestly functions: offering Holy Masses, celebrated at midnight where thousands of young men received Holy Communion, some for the last time."

Figure 6. German forces counterattack through the rubble-choked street of Warsaw. Source: Dni Powstania

Within a few hours after the eruption of the conflict, the Germans reacted with the rather limited forces at hand. The German Regular Army (Wehrmacht) in Warsaw numbered a minimum number of officers and a few thousand men. Sent immediately to curb the rebellion were two additional units, one called the Kaminski Brigade (1,700 men) and the other the Dirlewanger Brigade. Both were made up of the scum of the Germany armies. The Dirlewanger group consisted of prisoners released from jails to join the army. The Kaminski unit was an assortment of Ukrainian degenerates who saw the war in terms of pillage and riotous living. These groups at Warsaw left in their wake an untold amount of murder, rape, and robbery.

They were known to have shot up hospital wards and gunned down women and children. They stole from everyone, including regular army Germans. On one day alone, August 5th, some 10,000 civilians were murdered in an insane spree of violence. Dirlewanger, one of the most vicious men in the German Officer Corps, was known to be a sadist and a sexual pervert who had already spent time in German prisons. In Warsaw's history, no German units are remembered more vividly than these two groups. Their names are enshrined in the Polish collective memory as an examples of "pure evil." (Dirlewanger was recognized after the war by Polish ex-POWs in Germany. They beat him to death.)

Regular Army units soon arrived to put a degree of discipline into the German efforts. General Erich von dem Bach-Zelewski by August 5th, had assessed the situation and moved regular units into the areas surrounding the Home Army. (General von dem Bach, on entering the city, was appalled. Seeing the piles of civilian bodies, he said, "A military force that loots and massacres ceases to fight.") The commanding officer, von dem Bach, did not remove the offending brigades but in time had General Kaminski tried and executed and the Kaminski Brigade was soon disbanded.

German forces then began to systematically eliminate the Polish insurgents. An eventual 50,000 soldiers under at least a half-dozen generals would take part in the two-month battle. The opposing Home Army, which arose out of the basements and apartments of Warsaw, numbered only 40,000 men and women. They had 844 sub-machine guns with 121,000 rounds of ammunition, 46 heavy machine guns (150,000 rounds), 1,386 rifles and 5,000 grenades. One historian says, "The AK looked like a motley bunch, dressed in all sorts of clothing, some pre-war Polish military, some even confiscated SS outfits. The diversity in clothes was matched by an exotic collection of hats: Polish, German, and French."

The Germans, with the most up-to-date equipment, set about to destroy the hiding places of the Polish rebels. Their artillery began to blow apart buildings; tanks were brought into play—fifty Goliath tanks! The German Air Force bombed the affected areas. Huge cannon came into action, not only the famous German 88's, but six 150 mm guns, two 280 mm and two 300 mm howitzers. The German Army war log for August 15th records, "A new piece of equipment will arrive in Warsaw, 60 cm monster Karl." Polish books today record its effects. They too called the mammoth piece, mounted on railway cars, the "Karl."

During the very earliest days of the uprising, Fr. Paczek was moving back and forth, dodging German patrols, caring for the injured and dying wherever they might be found; he was at the hospitals and with the North Group. He often carried the Holy Sacrament. He sometimes had the Host wrapped in a larger loaf of bread. Later in the battle he would never leave the fighting area. He told his parishioners in North Dakota at a later date, carrying the Blessed Sacrament was "one of the happiest moments in the whole war."

Another memory that stayed with him through the years happened at the Red Cross Hospital as he was treating the wounded. He wrote, "I saw a young woman, a paramedic, on a stretcher. When she saw him she smiled and said, 'Chaplain, tell my parents that I am dying willingly, performing my duties to defend the liberty of my country and freedom of my religion.'"

Some arms were sent to the embattled Home Army by air. British and Polish flyers of the RAF tried, against great odds, to deliver weapons and ammunition by parachute. At least ten supply missions were flown. The casualty rate among the air crews was high. Historian Lukas says, "245 Poles, English, and South Africans were known to have been shot down." (One of the great scandals of the war was the Russian initial refusal to allow Allied planes to land at their airfields so "round trip" flights from England and Italy to Warsaw would not be necessary. Only in the last days of the battle did the Soviets allow such flights to land in their territory.) So some air assistance did come about. Whether with Russian help or not, on August 18th, 110 B-17 {Flying Fortresses] dropped 1,284 containers of ammunition and firearms. Yet, with hindsight, all accounts of the Uprising say the airborne assistance was too little and too late.

Figure 7. The burial of a Home Army comrade. Source: Dni Powstania

On one of these occasions, a low-flying British plane, circling to drop supplies, hit a chimney and its two sections came down in flames. They landed on the roofs of the Dluga 15 and Miodowa 16, Fr. Paczek's two places of residence. It was only with great exertion that flames on the roofs were quenched and the buildings were spared.

For the first Uprising days, the Red Cross Hospital, though damaged, was, to a certain extent, still operating. But soon the vicious SS troops, perhaps in the Kaminski Brigade, entered the building and began to plunder and take medical supplies. They were even prepared to execute the patients and the staff. A German-speaking physician negotiated with the reckless soldiers. A mass murder was avoided. Warsaw history records another brutal hospital massacre that occurred a few days later; it may have been the Red Cross Hospital, perhaps a nearby medical facility. Yet, in the initial stages of the Uprising, the Red Cross hospital had two sections, one for servicemen and the other for civilians. Eventually, however, the fighting spilled into the hospital area and the buildings were destroyed. Today, only a plaque marks its former site.

Fr. Paczek ("Germen") not only cared for the wounded and the dead, he was given the assignment of recording the time, place, and name of the deceased. In a still-existing underground headquarters order, "Germen," chief chaplain of the North Group, issued this edict (August 16, 1944):

I have ordered

1. The dead to be buried at the closest place, or at Dluga 15.

2. Duplicate copies of death certificates are to be made. In case of no identification, any documents must be put in bottles and buried with the corpse.

3. A continuous list of deaths must be made.

4. Chaplains are to have masses in the church or in some places at different times of the day.

Photographs taken during the Uprising show graves, with simple crosses, at assorted places: gardens, small parks, and even in solitary locations where soil could be found.

Numerous comments in modern Polish chronicles of the battle period say how fortunate it was that after hostilities people could identify the bodies of their loved ones and give them a proper burial. Certainly, much credit must be given to the chief chaplains of all the units, and for the North Group, especially to Fr. Paczek. August 16, 1944, was a busy day for Chief Chaplain "Germen." In case there was any doubt he issued more specific rules:

1. If someone is found dead in a street or distant from a cemetery, the body must be buried at that spot.

2. If a person dies in a hospital,

    (a) bury them in a military burial ground or on the hospital-grounds

    (b) They can also be buried at Garnizonowy Church.

Figure 8. Simple wooden crosses mark the graves of Polish casualties. Source: Powstanie Warszawskie

3. Any documents that can be found must be put in a bottle and buried with the body.

4. Two copies must be made of death certificate

   (a) By the chaplain or leader

   (b) In the hospital by medical people

5. A list of valuables, personal items, must be sent to the Chief Chaplain of the North Group.

In a tribute to Fr. Paczek given at a Home Army veterans gathering, a comment was made that because of the great number of casualties, "Germen's" orders could not always be followed. The orator said circumstances were not always as neat and orderly as Fr. Paczek would have hoped. In fact, the speaker told a priest friend in North Dakota that in one day they had 150 to 200 individuals to bury. It was necessary to dig a large hole "in front of the church" and bury people in a mass grave.

The burial of soldiers was not the only task given to Fr. Paczek. Several accounts say that he was to hide precious items in secret places under the floor (basement) of the Garnizonowy Church. (Years later, Polish authorities probably thanked, in their minds, the unnamed person who in battle saved at least parts of their special heritage.)

The Uprising cast the city of Warsaw into complete convulsions; chaos reigned everywhere. One member of the Canadian Combatants Association recorded in a quarterly publication:

> From day one of the insurrection the face of Warsaw changed and kept on changing. Some parts of the city were in our hands but large ones remained in the hands of the Germans who attacked the insurgents with planes, tanks and artillery. Main arteries were under fire and almost impossible to cross. More and more buildings came down as result of artillery fire and bombing. Barricades were built and underground passages were dug under the streets and across cellars to enable movement of troops and people without being exposed to the enemy fire.

"Germen" seemed to have displayed a remarkable sense of composure through all the violent moments. His commander, Colonel Karol Ziemski, said "the Dean (Chief Chaplain) is a man, calm, smiling, and without nerves." Fr. Paczek's immediate military superior Major Stanislaw Blaszczak ("Rog") remembered: "Our Dean was always there when we needed him most, in the first line, not with arms but with the Sacrament and prayers to help those who would say goodbye to the world."

The Garnizonowy Church, previously mentioned, was a landmark structure in the Old City. It was on Dluga, not far from Dluga 15 and the Red Cross Hospital. It

Figure 9. The Garnizonowy Church after destruction in Uprising battles. Source: Warsaw

was under its floors that "Germen" and other chaplains would often bury the dead. It was here, early in the Uprising, that the chaplains would offer nighttime Masses. War noises would probably die down after nightfall. The church, at least in the first days of the battle, was also the site of large gatherings of combatants as they received the news of the day and were apprised of future plans.

On one occasion, two companies of soldiers were lined up at the church door as an honor guard. Suddenly Fr. Paczek had a premonition of disaster. He ordered everyone into the church (perhaps it was into a subterranean area). As they got into "cover" a stream of artillery shells hit the church. The Germans knew they were there.

Figure 10. The Garnizonowy Church as restored today. Immediately to the left is Dluga 15 (Bishop Gawlina's residence; also Fr. Paczek's home). Five Jewish families were hidden in the top floor. Source: Warsaw

Figure 11. Insurgents met in the landmark Garnizonowy Church early in the uprising battle. Source: Powstanie Warszawskie

Eugeniusz Melech, in his famous diary of Uprising events, wrote:

> I want to go to Church, but where? All churches are shut and under German shooting. Masses are celebrated by our clergymen in cellars, in private lodgings, in courtyards and in other safe places. The chaplains celebrate Masses, they have much work for they celebrate several Masses, because many are killed. Our clergy is very patriotic [with] confessions, weddings, and burials of killed soldiers and people. Very often, the Germans through their spies get information where there are these great concentrations of faithful people who want to take part in Mass. On them the Germans begin their deadly shooting.

Casting more light on these "concentrations" of people, Fr. Paczek in his 1986 Polish booklet, wrote: "We had a movie theater in our besieged part of town. At night the theater was turned into a house of worship where officers and men would gather for Mass. There they would pray and sing patriotic songs."

The Garnizonowy Church was soon central to much of the fighting. Fr. Paczek, writing to a Polish scholar several decades after the war, said that by August 15, the chapel in Bishop Gawlina's residence, Dluga 15, was in ruins. That meant Fr. Paczek and his fellow Pallottines had to seek refuge elsewhere. He adds a note saying that by August 20 the Garnizonowy Church was "so destroyed that it couldn't be used at all."

The membership of the Warsaw Uprising Army, at least in the North Group, included a large number of very young men. A glance at photographs taken during the struggle will inevitably elicit the comment, "So many are so young," and it was true. Many soldiers were college students. In fact, some were adolescents, senior members of the Polish Boy Scouts. Accordingly, one of Fr. Paczek's titles was "Chaplain to the 36th Regiment of Academic Infantry." The presence of these young men may have been because the North Group was situated in an area close to the University. It was in an academic part of town.

Figure 12. College students and scouts, learning the use of military weapons. Source: Dni Powstania

It wasn't just men who participated in the Uprising. Some young women carried arms. The medical profession, of course, was present with many nurses and female medical assistants. There was even a contingent of female paramedics. Fr. Paczek had

Figure 13. Women paramedics worked to care for the wounded. Source: Dni Powstania

been involved in the hospital training of these young women before the hostilities. He certainly knew many personally and worked closely with them in the perilous battle situations.

One frightful day when Fr. Paczek was near exhaustion, he worked his way up to the fifth floor of a downtown building. He recalled in his small memoir booklet an event which surely was one of those occasions in which the "Virgin Mary saved my life." He had just closed his eyes in sleep when there was the very loud rushing sound of an artillery shell. It was close, but had not exploded and when the dust settled it turned out to be a monster projectile. Apparently there was nothing in the way to activate the fuse device. Fr. Paczek wrote, "It was then I heard a voice saying, 'Father Chaplain, get out of there or you'll disappear just like Twardowski on the moon.'" (There was a Polish folk tale about a man named Twardowski who, because of his pranks, ended up on the moon.) Fr. Paczek never knew where the voice came from, but he ran from the big shell all the way to the basement. (Photos still exist of the huge-unexploded projectile, 600 mm in diameter [over two feet], one discharged from a railroad car platform.) Later Fr. Paczek came across men taking the shell apart to extract the powder for use in making grenades. He told the soldiers doing the work that they were "very brave." They, in return, gave him a souvenir as a reminder of the event. It was a rabbit foot. He was very "lucky."

Fr. Paczek, "Germen" to the authorities, received more than a rabbit's foot for his valor. At the beginning of the Uprising, on August 8, 1944 (Military Order No. 18), he had been presented with the medal *Krzyz Walecznych* (Valiant Cross). Before the month was complete he received a second award, the medal *Zloty Krzyz z Mieczami* (Golden Cross of Merit With Sabres).

Figure 14. Salvaging explosive from an unexploded German artillery projectile.
Source: Dni Powstania

Not to be outdone, Fr. Major "Germen" recommended the award of the *Krzyz Walecznych* Medal to other chaplains in the North Group command. This recommendation, in its original handwriting, was found in a Warsaw Archive. The chaplains were listed by their pseudonyms: "Wisna" and "Jakub." It was signed simply "Germen."

Another North Group underground document recently came to light in the London Free Poland archives. On August 24, 1944, Fr. Paczek recommended that the Medal *Krzyz Walecznych* be given to five chaplains in his charge: Fr. "Dardzinski" (pseudonym) "killed taking care of the wounded"; and Fr. "Rogozinski," wounded on the barricades, also Fr. "Lukas," Fr. "Michal," and Fr. "Andrzej," all of whom had displayed great heroism in caring for the injured. The document was also signed "Germen." With this historic record we can see that Fr. Paczek was involved in some very deadly events: two of his own priest-chaplains were casualties, one dead and another wounded.

An underground communiqué, also found in post-war Warsaw, says, "On this day, September 17, 1944, the rank of major is awarded to Captain "Germen" of Grupa Polnoc (North Group). It is signed by Home Army General and overall commander "Monter."

CHAPTER FOUR

Surrender

IT MUST BE REMEMBERED that close to 40,000 Poles were involved in the Warsaw Uprising, and the majority were irregulars, highly motivated but not professional soldiers. At the end of that two-month period, 50,000 German soldiers, often seasoned veterans with years of combat, were facing the insurgent Poles. These soldiers had the best of modern weapons.

Negotiations were being carried out with the German commander, General Erich von dem Bach-Zelewski, regarding an end of hostilities in the central part of the city. All the while, fighting continued. Food supplies were desperately limited, power was shut off, ammunition was almost exhausted, and the number of wounded was steadily increasing. The situation was getting desperate. Colonel Ziemski had already consolidated the areas under his command. In groups, his soldiers made their way to strong points in strategic areas.

In a tribute to Fr. Paczek in 1971, a Polish veteran of the battles mentioned "Germen's" movement through what in Polish is called "the canals," but in English is a not-so-refined word: sewers. Indeed, the sewer system of the Old Town was a major communication link for soldiers of the North Group. Home Army soldiers, civilians, and even German prisoners were moved from place to place as the need arose. One participant later described the vile journeys: "Sometimes it required hours of walking, often bent down through noxious gases and sludge. People emerging from the man holes required cleaning and medical help." An historian mentions that the Germans discovered some of the underground pathways and "full scale battles took place in the subterranean mazes. There were hand-to-hand fights in the excrement."

To his credit, General von dem Bach, the German commander, tried various ways to end the conflict with times of truce, pleas for the safety of Warsaw's civilians, and even using clergy as mediators. (The Catholic Archbishop was involved.) The Swiss Red Cross representatives were on hand and they inspected the prison camps with their housing, medical facilities and food allotments.

The assault on the Old Town began with a special intensity on August 19th and went on until the 2nd of September. Some 4,000 tons of shells fell into Home Army area, a region only a square mile in size. Out of the 1,100 buildings in Polish hands, 400 were completely destroyed and 300 were badly burned. Eventually the struggle in the Old Town became

Figure 15. Surrender talks through a lady intermediary. Source: Dni Powstania

impossible. Richard Lukas says, "On the night of September 1, 1,500 soldiers, 500 civilians, and 100 German prisoners began the 1,700-yard trek through the [sewer] slime." Fr. Paczek was with them. They moved to a final defensive area in Zoliborz. Here the full weight of German forces came into play. Time was running out. The Soviet Army did not enter the battle and Allied air support was of little consequence.

One by one the various Home Army sectors were forced to capitulate. The Mokotow enclave fell on September 17th. Fr. Wincenty Marozuk offered the last Mass in Zoliborz on September 29th.

Polish commander Bor had to make a most difficult decision. By September 29, he sent an envoy to the German General von dem Bach, who had promised in the name of the German military that the surrendered Home Army soldiers would be treated as prisoners of war, according to the Geneva Conventions. The British, in particular, had previously insisted that the German government should treat the Warsaw Polish combatants according to that Convention, which Germany had signed in 1928. The British probably reminded Germany that several hundred thousand of their own soldiers were in Allied prisoner of war camps.

By October 2, details had been worked out and on October 5th, General Bor left the rubble and went out to meet his counterpart, General von dem Bach. The Uprising was over.

The official history of the Polish Armed Forces estimated there were 21,600 casualties in the Warsaw struggle: 10,000 dead, 6,600 wounded, and 5,000 missing in action. On the German side, one authoritative source says there were 26,000 casualties and of that number, about 10,000 were killed, 7,000 were missing, and 9,000 suffered wounds. Civilian casualties in Warsaw were unbelievably high, over 200,000 men, women, and children were killed or murdered. The Uprising, for the Poles in Warsaw, was a truly horrendous event.

Fr. Paczek, following the lead of his unit commanders, Colonel Karol "Wachonowski" Ziemski and Major Stanislaw "Rog" Blaszczak, was part of the surrendering troops. In the later years of his life he would speak of his North Group as "one of the toughest." And he was probably right. Polish histories of the Uprising give his unit a special place in their accounts.

The German soldiers, no longer the riffraff of the first days of the battle, were now regular army men. They treated the wretched looking "survivors" with respect.

(They knew also that the Germans captured by the insurgents had been properly cared for, according to the Geneva Code.)

Reports say that at least some of the Germans saluted as the surrendering Poles assembled after emerging from the devastated buildings. Trying as best they could, the Poles stood erect and in precision during the surrender event. According to Fr. Paczek, they deposited their weapons, saluted, and walked back to their ranks. One account said General Bor led them as they sang the Polish anthem, which starts with the line, "Poland Is Not Yet Dead."

This is not the end of the story. Among the few incidents Fr. Paczek would tell is one that occurred at the surrender time. A high-ranking German officer (a general), seeing he was a chaplain, approached Fr. Paczek, and looking over the Home Army "veterans" with a serious expression on his face, questioned him. "What kind of soldiers are these? They seem to be students and even Boy Scouts." Fr. Paczek answered, "Yes, sir, it's true, and we lost a lot of them." The officer turned away with tears

Figure 16. Student member of Home Army. Source: Dni Powstania

Figure 17. Remains of Warwaw's Market Square. Source: Warsaw

streaming from his eyes. After a few moments he said, "I have two sons (nephews ?) who just completed their academic studies. Right now they are fighting on the Eastern (Russian) front. I wonder if they will ever come back." Fr. Paczek assured the officer, "Sir, everything is in God's hands. At a time like this we must have deep faith." "Thank you Chaplain," the officer said and the words burst from his mouth.

"Our hearts were aching when we were leaving destroyed Warsaw," Fr. Paczek, in his Polish booklet, wrote. "Soldiers had tears in their eyes as they looked at the sea of rubble and debris." And they would have been more saddened if they had known what the future had in store for their beloved city. Hitler, in an act of vengeance, ordered that Warsaw be razed! destroyed! And with German efficiency they did just that. All of the inhabitants of the city were removed. Special military units

Figure 18. Marching to Ozarow railroad station from Zolidorz after surrender
Source: Dni Powstania

were brought in; with explosives and flamethrowers they "torched" the city.

Several weeks later Warsaw became a battleground again when the Soviets, after their long delay, crossed the Vistula and took over the city. In many ways they were "liberating" an already uninhabited town.

It is said that eighty-five, maybe ninety percent of the city was destroyed. It was a metropolitan area filled with architectural marvels, and home to over a million people. After the war, some suggested that it would be cheaper to completely raze the city and to build a new Warsaw on an open plain some miles away. Polish national pride and good sense prevailed. No such a thing took place. From old drawings, photographs, and from collective memories, the city (at least the Old Town) was rebuilt. It stands today as a thing of great beauty and an attraction to many tourists. (Part of the modern "tour" of the city are the memorials to the heroes of the great battle of Warsaw.)

For the veterans of the Uprising, the surrender was the beginning of another set of hardships. They were marched seven miles to the suburban town of Ozarow. There they were crowded into wooden freight cars and sent off on a journey to prisoner of war camps in Germany.

CHAPTER FIVE
To the POW Camp

THE HOME ARMY INSURGENTS apparently spent several days at Ozarow. There was confusion among the German authorities. Germany had special camps spread throughout their country: POW camps for Allied prisoners, detention camps, concentration camps for political prisoners, and death camps for extermination. What would they do for these unique Geneva Convention Polish prisoners? From the beginning it was determined that men of the higher ranks would be separated from the ordinary privates and sergeants.

The word went out that Fr. Paczek's unit, the North Group, would go to Bergen-Belsen in north Germany. That name might have struck fear in their hearts for Bergen-Belsen was a camp with a sinister reputation. Its function changed through the war years. It had been a detention and often an execution camp for women and handicapped prisoners; it was also a transit camp, and in the last months of the war it became a full-fledged death camp. (This happened, however, after the Poles had been moved.) After the war it was determined some 48,000 to 50,000 had been killed on its premises; Jews were often sent there on the way to Auschwitz. A photograph exists showing General D. Eisenhower looking with anger at piles of Bergen-Belsen's dead bodies.

Fr. Paczek wrote later that the disquieting thought came to them that Bergen-Belsen was a "revenge" camp because their North Group battalion was responsible, under "Rog," and "Wachonowski" for giving Germans such a beating. They were taking us to the concentration camp to liquidate us!

Figure 19. Loading at Ozarow railroad station after surrender. Source: Dni Powstania

In the North Group battles and subsequently on the journey to the POW camp was an individual named Jan Dobraczynski. Like others, he had a pseudonym, "Eugeniuse." This man, a writer by profession, was head of the unit's Information and Propaganda Section—the ones who published newspapers, posters, and other printed material. Jan Dobraczynski (whose writings made him a popular Polish post-war figure) published a volume detailing his war experiences: *Gra w Wybijanego.* Fr. Paczek appears, at times, in the account. Dobraczynski's pages give us a glimpse of the captivity period: September 1944 to May 1945.

The train (or trains), once they started from Ozarow, took the prisoners across the border, through Frankfurt am Oder, and from there to the transportation hub of Berlin. (The Allied bombers had not yet devastated the city; that would come later!) From Berlin the train traveled north and west. They were lucky; they escaped the Allied fighter-bombers, which were ranging all over the countryside, seeking especially Germany's rail transport system. Jan Dobraczynski remembers stopping at a small railroad station in Warthegau. Here they were allowed to leave the cars to gather potatoes from a nearby field. (They marched, according to Dobraczynski, to and from the field in a brisk formation fashion. One individual even displayed a small Polish flag.) On this occasion, he said, some women gave them bread and the German guards provided a meal.

As the train approached Bergen-Belsen, Fr. Paczek wrote, they stopped to spend a night. The men were convinced the Germans would not keep the capitulation agreement and would perhaps kill them. Colonel Ziemski ordered that a document be compiled with the names of each captive inscribed. This list would be, somehow, given to the International Red Cross. It would be a kind of "insurance policy" to deter the Germans in case they had extermination in mind.

Fr. Paczek wrote in his little Polish-language booklet, "The next day we entered the camp, and there appeared a delegation from the Red Cross with regulations concerning the treatment of prisoners of war. Among the Germans, this was a big surprise, for whatever plans they may have had, they were exposed [sic]."

Apparently many of the signs of the Bergen-Belsen camp's harsh period had been removed. Post-war prisoner accounts never mention such things. Yet there must have been a kind of brooding atmosphere in the place, an awareness of the dreadful things that had occurred and would again occur at that fateful site.

Jan Dobraczynski remembered the camp was divided into subdivisions, six barracks to each unit, with barbed wire around the various compounds. Jan was with Fr. Paczek in the section containing barracks numbers 196-201. One room in one of the barracks was designated as a chapel. Eventually Mass was held each day at 10 a.m. Once a week the inmates could shave and periodically their clothes were sent to an "oven" to be disinfected.

So there was a religious dimension to their prisoner days. Besides Fr. Paczek, other priests, it seems, were in the Bergen-Belsen camp. Listed prominently is Fr.

(Lt. Col.) Jan Wojciechowski ("Koreb"). The Polish soldiers were devout and certainly some of their German guards were religious people. War has a way of bringing men to the more fundamental things of life. For the Germans, with Russian armies approaching, religion was probably becoming even more important.

By January 1945, a sense of desperation was beginning to appear in German military circles. The Allies (Americans, British, and French—with some Free Polish units) had recovered from the Battle of the Bulge and were already on the Rhine River. The Soviets had overcome Warsaw and were moving across Poland into the Baltic countries. All over Germany there was a shifting of people and materials. Foodstuffs were becoming even scarcer and the vaunted German discipline was starting to show signs of distress.

The Bergen-Belsen area was affected. One mid-January day the prisoners were told to gather their things, were lined up, and then forced to set off on a great march that would take them to the north, to a more remote area in Scheswig-Holstein. Trains took them an initial 10 km to Fallingbostel and Gross-Born. From there they were to walk 150 km (100 miles) to Sandbostel near the German city of Lubeck.

The long, wintertime march, for the already undernourished prisoners, was a frightful experience. A fellow prisoner, Stanislaw Podlewski, recorded incidents along the way: "As we were about to pass German search areas, we would bury our personal items, then dig them up after the search. German guards would steal whatever we possessed."

Post-war reports say at least 100,000 Allied POWs in this same time period were being moved on foot in Germany to keep them from Russian and Anglo armies. Starved and sick, thousands died in the process.

Everywhere there were signs of confusion among the German public and even the military personnel. Jan Dobraczynski wrote that they came upon a wounded Belgian soldier, in fact, an SS soldier. Dobraczynski, who could talk French, spent a moment with him in conversation. The soldier was so happy he gave Dobraczyski, out of gratitude, a grenade. When the German guard saw it he said, "Where did you get it?" "From a wounded soldier," he replied, and smiled: "I'll keep it as a souvenir. I'll put it on my desk." The guard was upset. He said, "Please give it to me. If they catch you with it, they will shoot me, and you too."

The long lines of Polish prisoners, after the two-month winter journey, finally arrived at the Sandbostel camp. It turned out to be a frightfully overcrowded place. By this time they were joined with officer-prisoners from other European armies; several of these Allied units had priests of their own with them.

Again, the men set up their internal camp procedures: elementary sanitation, medical facilities, food and religious programs. A total of four Polish priests were there. Fr. Paczek was second in rank under Fr. Jan Wojciechowski. American food parcels arrived on occasion. These were distributed by the International Red Cross. Jan Dobraczynski wrote that he was very sick, with a leg wound and serious fever. He says that with the arrival of the food parcels, he was restored to his normal healthy condition.

Dobraczynski, in his book *Gra w Wybijanego,* says:

> Food packages from America saved us from starvation, but not from the cold. Every barracks had its own stove-heater, but the Germans said there was no fuel for us. They came up with a proposal: they would divide us into small groups and we would go to nearby forests and get our own fuel. They would send only one guard with each group. They emphasized that if anyone escaped, it would be the end of the agreement. One did later escape to Poland, two got to Holland. That eventually ended the arrangement.

Easter services were held, bringing memories of home to the thousands crammed inside the prison's barbed wire. The great majority of prisoners were Catholic. The Polish priests, with a priest from France, Italy, and Yugoslavia, had Mass with as much ceremony as possible, even a procession with a monstrance and the Holy Sacrament.

War was coming to an end. Spirits lightened and a sense of humor began to surface. Dobraczynski wrote in his book:

> We had in our camp a sympathetic and rather fat officer (Lieutenant? Captain?) who had formerly been a restaurant owner in Hanover. This man was appointed as commandant of the camp. He was surprised at his promotion. He explained with great enthusiasm that even though he was not the highest ranking officer, he was still in charge and that now he had the right to carry an officer's ceremonial dagger. We couldn't complain about the commander. He helped us as much as he could.

Rumors of liberation were in the air. The prisoners could every day hear the sounds of Allied aircraft overhead, on their way to bring destruction to German cities and military installations. The guards became very relaxed, even letting small groups go into the countryside to gather food. The camp commander told the prisoners, "You can leave if you wish," but advised against it. "In the confusion of the moment, someone may shoot you."

On the second day of May, a shout went up. British tanks could be seen coming down the Hamburg-Lubeck Highway. Armored cars and British soldiers soon appeared. The German guards were rounded up. Now the Poles knew they were no longer prisoners, but were free and very happy men.

Amid all the rejoicing, thoughts of God filled the minds of most of the grateful men. The next day, May 3rd, happened to be one of their great national holidays: the Feast Day of Mary, Queen of Poland. An altar was erected in the camp's central square. Fr. Paczek recalled, years later, the "sea of faces" as he and the other priests celebrated Mass amid tears and cheers. It was the end of a terrible ordeal. They would all be alive. They could breathe again the air of freedom.

CHAPTER SIX

Displaced Persons Camps

THE LUBECK-SANBOSTEL AREA in the northwestern part of Germany, by agreement among the Allies, fell into the British Occupation Zone. The British military authorities wasted no time in setting up an efficient camp structure. They had a special force of administrators and camp police. (The designation was strange to American ears: The Watchman's Service.) Senior Polish officers were identified and officially put in charge; medical and food matters were taken care of, and mail and notification of families was expedited. The Polish themselves handled most organizational matters. The world for the former prisoners began to fall into its proper perspective.

Almost immediately, Fr. Paczek's friend from the fighting days, Colonel Karol Ziemski, was recognized as camp commander. Contact was made with other Polish military groups, but not with the Polish Communist government located in Lublin, Poland. The Polish Free Government in London was kept abreast of the situation, although the Allied governments were forced to recognize the Soviet-led Lublin government. (They had no choice, for Russian armies controlled Warsaw and all the rest of that country.)

From the beginning the priests at the camp got into communication with their own ecclesiastical superiors. The Vatican had already set in place a Monsignor Edward Lubowiecki, one of the approximately 4000 Polish priests who had been in the Dachau concentration camp. This gentleman served as Vicar General for all the Polish Catholics in Germany. Soon to visit the camps in Fr. Paczek's area was

Figure 20. After liberation: Sanbostel camp officers
Left front: Colonel Karol "Wachonowski," Ziemski
Right front: Major Stanislaw "Rog" Blaszczak
Back row right: Fr. Major V. Paczek

the Chief Bishop of all the Poles in American, French, and British zones, Bishop Josef Gawlina. He must have been welcomed as a great friend for he had been a bishop in Warsaw. It was, in fact, his house next to the Garnizonowy Church (Dluga 15) in which Fr. Paczek and the Pallottines had lived until its destruction in the Uprising. Bishop Gawlina had been an active anti-German spokesman. He was thus forced to leave his country and spent the war taking care of Free Polish armies in England, Africa, and Italy.

With the fall of Germany, Polish conscripted laborers and inmates of concentration camps began to surface all over the German countryside, well over 100,000 in the British zone alone. There was the expected end-of-the-war confusion: how to feed and house them? Ultimately to answer the questions: who wanted to return to Poland? Who dared not return to Poland? Who wished to go to free countries like England, the United States, Canada, and Australia? What countries would allow them in? The term "displaced persons" ("D.P.s") came into existence. It would take years to sort it all out. (Every state, almost every town in the United States would eventually receive homeless D.P. people from one or another subjugated European country).

One of the problems for Germany's displaced Polish citizens was their awareness of the atheistic Communist regime that had taken over their government. It was a regime kept in place by Russians. And the Poles were understandably wary of Russians. They recalled the Soviet invasion of their eastern borders and the deportation of one-and-a-half million of their civilians and soldiers. They knew of the murder of 5,000 of their officers at the Katyn Forest.

The Poles in German exile knew also that alongside the Home Army had been what the Communists called the Underground Peoples Army. This relatively smaller group had been of little help during the Uprising but at the end of the war had received almost all the credit for the liberation. History was being rewritten and the Home Army was not part of it. Veterans of the Warsaw Uprising and its accompanying "risings" elsewhere were forced to keep silent, some actually jailed and all suffered discrimination.

The hundreds of thousands of Polish airmen, soldiers, and sailors who fought with the Allies were literally "men without a country." No wonder after the war associations of Home Army veterans existed only in such countries as America, Britain, Canada, and Australia.

Jan Dobraczynski in describing his prison camp life *(Gra w Wydijanego)* recalled now he discussed with Fr. Paczek his indecision as to whether to return to his homeland or stay in the free world West. Fr. Paczek advised a return to Poland, which he did. As mentioned previously, Dobraczynski eventually became one of Poland's most celebrated post-war authors; some of his books were translated into English.

All the displaced persons' civil affairs were handled, of course, through British military and governmental offices. Church matters were different and it was here that people like Fr. Paczek came into play. For the British administrative district, Colonel Karol Ziemski was appointed the Senior Polish officer in the Schleswig-

Holstein region. He, in turn, made Fr. Major Jan Wojciechowski Chief Chaplain of what was known as the 30th British Corps area. Fr. Major Valerian Paczek, already involved with refugees, on March 7, 1946, was officially appointed by Colonel Ziemski as Senior Chaplain for the British 8th Corps in Schleswig-Holstein.

There were, at the end of hostilities, 280,000 Poles in Germany. It was soon determined that a large proportion (close to 150,000) of those could be found in northern Germany. Caring for these individuals, predominantly Catholic in background, was an almost bewildering task. Women and children were involved, for the German war industry took its workers wherever they could be found.

A dozen camps were set up by British authorities, often using old German military installations. These camps provided initial lodging, food, medicine, and clothing. In time, more of the amenities of life were provided. In Schleswig-Holstein, camps arose at Lubeck, Rumpel, Fahrenberg, Sattenfeld, Grabau, Borstel, Idstedt, Wentorf, Wahlstedt, Sulfeld, and Bad Odesloe. (This is only a partial list.) Fr. Paczek, as Senior Chaplain, found himself responsible for the religious life of the civilians and thousands of ex-soldiers in these diverse camp facilities.

Starting with the handful of Polish "end-of-hostilities" priests at Sandbostel, Fr. Paczek probably breathed a sigh of relief when there appeared from all over Germany, 39 displaced Polish priests, some from labor camps, but most from concentration camps. His task was then to ascertain the status of the various priests, to determine their health and mental state, and then "put them to work." As Senior Chief Chaplain (they called him the Dean), he assigned them to each of the dozen camps listed above.

Well aware of military procedures and the traditional German respect for official positions, Fr. Paczek had each priest given a proper uniform, proper credentials, a salary, and the rank of Captain. He used the old adage, "Rank has its privileges."

In December 1946, Fr. Paczek wrote and had published a 110-page book entitled *Duszpasterstwo Polskiego Okregu Wojskowego*. It was published in Schleswig-Holstein and concerned Polish chaplains in the British 8th Corps area. This volume

Figure 21. Fr. Paczek and his ex-prisoner chaplains. Fr. Joseph Mentel is the tall man in back row.

is, indeed, of historical significance. The enormous scope of the chaplains' work (with photos) is detailed and biographical sketches are presented concerning almost every one of the priests involved in the "displaced person" work.

There were 39 priests in Fr. Paczek's book. Twenty-four were ex-prisoners from the dreaded Dachau. (One priest in the booklet *Fare Thee Well,* a survivor of Dachau, said of the 23 priests sent to Dachau from his Polish diocese, he and two others got out alive.) Ten of Fr. Paczek's chaplain-priests came from other concentration camps. The rest had probably an equally horrendous past: labor camps and the like. (Fr. Paczek, the author, omits any discussion of his own personal experiences.)

Just two examples from his *Duszpasterstwo* can be given: Fr. Alfons Szczepanski, born in 1906, was arrested on October 15, 1939. He was sent to concentration camps at Stutthof, Grenzdorf, Sachsenhausen, and finally to Dachau. The account says that after five years of "starvation and suffering" he was liberated April 29, 1945. Under Fr. Paczek he was caring for 1,200 Polish people in five different locations.

One priest in Fr. Paczek's book is of special interest to North Dakota people: Fr. Joseph Mentel, long-time pastor at St. Andrew's parish in Zeeland, North Dakota, and St. Philip's parish in Napoleon, North Dakota. Born in Szopience, Poland, he was ordained in 1940. With 42 priests in his diocese, he was taken into Western Germany and put to work at a variety of places including German-occupied Denmark. Work in Germany was hard. Fr. Mentel said in the *Fare Thee Well* booklet, "Some priests died from sickness and overwork." He worked as a medic very often and was himself wounded. Reticent about his conscripted labor years, he said, "We were glad to be alive to do our priestly work, secretly to even find a place to say Mass." In the camps in Scheswig-Holstein he met Archbishop A. Muench, the Vatican's official representative to Germany's Occupying Forces (later Apostolic Delegate). Bishop Muench recruited him for the Fargo Diocese where they needed priests who could "take care of German parishes."

An Aside: Looking over the names and backgrounds of the survivor-priests in Fr. Paczek's charge, one wonders how often in the history of the Church did so many truly heroic priests gather in one spot. Survivors of the worst oppression that modern society can inflict, and yet ready, without complaint, to help God's people wherever they could be found. The early Church had names for such people: "confessors." They experienced, what was called "White Martyrdom." No wonder Fr. Paczek, a very busy man who was also a student of history, went to great pains to record their story for posterity.

The approximate 150,000 Polish "displaced persons" for whom Fr. Paczek was responsible, as mentioned, were not just men, but included women and children. They were scattered over a large war-torn piece of territory. The administrative work, the supervisory tasks, in those confusing times, the weight of it all, would cause the most durable bishop to shudder. Yet Fr. Paczek saw himself a simple priest, trying to do his duty.

With the help of devout Polish men and women, the priest-chaplains found space and personnel to organize among the ex-prisoners an eventual three high schools and 25 grade schools. Whole buildings were taken over; makeshift churches came into being. Photographs exist that show surprisingly large classes of boys and girls, all in white, lined up for their First Communions. Other photos show Confirmation events with the young people waiting for a visiting bishop.

Weddings took place at a phenomenal rate. In 1945, from May to October, the priest-chaplains performed 1,903 weddings. (Fr. Paczek himself presided over 600—an unbelievable number). The priests together, during that time period, baptized 574 individuals, buried 218, and had 1,006 First Communions. The totals above are recorded in Fr. Paczek's *Duszpasterstwo* book.

Another Aside: The reader versed in the history of Catholic ceremonial laws, or for that matter Catholic Canon Law, will have occasion in the previous pages to wonder about certain wartime practices. In the days before and during the Uprising, a priest was normally allowed to offer only one Mass a day, and there was no such a thing as an afternoon or evening Mass. Yet we find the Polish chaplains offering Masses here and there and around the clock. In those pre-Vatican Council times, a communicant would fast from food from midnight the previous day. What of the underground afternoon and evening circumstances? What of the rule: no meat on Friday? What of the priest requirement to get "faculties" from a local bishop for hearing confessions when there was no local bishop?

If Fr. Paczek performed 600 weddings in a half year, what of baptismal certificates, instructions, banns and dispensations? Of particular interest, how could Fr. Paczek verify the "good standing" of priests who suddenly appeared after years in concentration camps?

The list could go on. What of Fr. Paczek with a cyanide capsule? In addition, we must remember that a priest in those days, as today, was not supposed to carry arms in combat, yet Fr. Paczek, with a 12-cartridge pistol, was going to "take twelve Russians with him" if he were captured a third time.

This writer is not a theologian, and Fr. Paczek was not a reckless cleric; he knew what he was doing. There are, thank God, in Church law, some provisions which say, in effect, "When the chips are down, within reason do whatever is needed." Is it called "Epieikeia" or "Ecclesia Supplet"? (For further details, ask your pastor, not this writer!)

Back to the story. In Fr. Paczek's post-war files there can be found several dozen papers which give us a sense of his busy life as an administrator working between the military, the German public, the church hierarchy, and the impatient ex-prisoners under his charge. One example, dated January 1, 1946, says, "This is to certify that the bearer, Rev. Major Paczek, Walerian, is acting as Dean to PWX and PP camps in the area of the 8 Corp, British Army. All military authorities are kindly requested to grant him the necessary assistance in performing his duty."

Sometimes the certificates allowed him a broad range of freedom in his tasks. August 31, 1946, he received this Duty Pass: "Paczek, W., Major, (Staff Chaplain) has permission to be absent from his unit for the purpose of inspection and visitation of chaplains on duty. He is authorized to be in BAOR area for thirty days, until 30 Sept. 1946. Means of transportation: car."

Sometimes the permissions are rather mundane: "This is to certify that Rev. Paczek, Walerian, Polish Senior Chaplain, RC, CMLO/CMVS, is authorized to carry 1,000 cigarettes for Polish chaplains RC CMLO/CMWS as a gift of the Relief Society for Poles in London."

Authorization documents, in four different languages, were found in Fr. Paczek's personal possessions: driver's licenses, identity certificates, medical records, permissions to move through various sectors and character acknowledgements.

It was a busy time, those first years after the war. Within that period (1946) he was made a regular officer in the Polish Army; prior to that he apparently held a kind of reserve status. On June 10, 1947, he became officially a part of the British Army, which must have meant he was treated and remunerated according to the British Army officer schedules.

Figure 22. Receiving commendation from British Imperial General Staff, 1948.

The Polish Free Government in London was very much aware of Fr. Paczek's activities. On September 15, 1945, he received a personal, hand-signed commendation from General Komorowski, the great "Bor" of the Underground Army years. (General "Bor," in today's Poland, is a national hero comparable to America's General MacArthur and General Eisenhower.) In his file, too, is a signed commendation from General W. Anders, the hero of Free World Polish forces.

The English, too, were grateful. On August 9, 1949, he received this citation from the British War Office: "Your name has been brought to the notice of the Chief of the Imperial General Staff and I am authorized by him to signify, by the award to you of this testimonial, his appreciation of the good service which you have rendered." Signed: Military Secretary—given to "Lieutenant Colonel Paczek."

Friends of Fr. Paczek said this recognition of the British government was presented to him on an occasion in which the Queen herself was present. In fact, at the reception afterward, the Queen noticed Fr. Paczek was drinking tea in his champagne glass. She said to him, "You are very wise, drink can be harmful."

What does this recognition by the British government mean? Does it add credence to the story that he was trained by the British to drop by parachute in the war period on one? two? occasions? Did he actually do such a thing? In 1948, the records of British wartime "undercover" activities were still secret. Any citation concerning such behind-the-scenes events would not have revealed specific information.

The nature of his post-war work in Germany was changing. Fr. Paczek, writing about his activities, says there was a gradual clarification of the status of the ex-prisoners. One by one, decisions were made. "After two years," he says, "many did return to Poland." Many, perhaps most, chose to remain in the "West." Allied government programs were proceeding as quickly as possible in placing the refugees in permanent lands and permanent homes in a half-dozen countries.

The Communist-led government in Poland was beginning to assert itself on the international scene. The "Cold War" was becoming a reality. No one in the West wanted to see Communism continue to expand further into Europe, certainly not the Polish ex-soldiers who refused to return to the oppressive world behind the Iron Curtain. True to his character, Fr. Paczek joined the struggle. On at least two occasions he broadcast, in Polish, speeches on Radio Free Europe in which he emphasized the need for civil and religious freedoms. In doing so, he certainly realized he became an enemy of the Polish state. He became a "marked man" and if he returned to his homeland he could be put in prison (and, in fact, he never would again set foot on the soil of the country he fought so hard to liberate). Not only was he to become a permanent exile, he became a "non-person." Rarely was his name mentioned in accounts of the war written in Poland during the first decades of Communist government control.

Not surprisingly, the jurisdiction of the Polish Free Government in London began to change. On June 17, 1947, he was officially "released from the Polish Armed Services." The document was signed by his friend, Colonel Karol Ziemski. He, no doubt, reverted again to his former reserve officer status for the London government would eventually elevate him to the rank of Lt. Colonel and eventually to full Colonel.

His duties in Germany would continue, however, for the British government officially appointed him in January 1947 as Chief Chaplain of The Watchman's Service and Transport Companies in the British zone of Germany. Now with his status assured he did much of the same relief work. In fact, on November 23, 1949, he was appointed Director of all the "Caritas" welfare work in the British occupation areas.

The Polish people in his charge, by the third year after the war, had diminished greatly in number. One by one, the "refugee" priests had obtained permanent assignments; many went to parishes in the United States and Canada. (Their service time under British auspices had already given them a certain fluency in English.)

Fr. Paczek was a Pallottine priest. In all of his activities, both in Poland and in Germany, he had worked with the permission of his religious superiors. The situation among Pallottines in Poland was understandably confusing in the immediate post-war period. The Pallottine headquarters in Rome was still intact. Apparently the Superior General, sometime after the cessation of hostilities, set up a special Pallottine organization in France to give the Polish priests some authoritative center until their futures could be determined. Fr. Paczek, thereby, sought his direction from the Pallottine officials in Paris.

Knowing that he could not return to Poland, and realizing his work in Germany was coming to an end, Fr. Paczek, already comfortable in an English-speaking world, began to look to the United States. He notified his British authorities and his service to Her Majesty's military ended officially on March 21, 1950.

The commanding officer at the English staff at Osnabreuk, Germany, wrote on May 15, 1950:

> I find it difficult to report adequately on the excellent work Father Paczek carried out. His influence and control over his countrymen living in exile in Germany is beyond all praise. ... The help he has given to the British authorities will always be remembered. Father Paczek is a man of great dignity, high ideals, fine intelligence...great loyalty to his work. ... [He was] especially successful in his relationship to all British officers [who] feel keenly his departure.

In just a few lines, Fr. Paczek wrote of his movement to America, "In May 1950, I was ordered by my General to go to the USA, Buffalo, New York, to help organize a Polish Province of The Society of the Catholic Apostolate" (Pallottines). But it was not as simple as that. His personal files show permissions and personal resumes in three different languages. His application to emigrate involved a certain amount of paperwork, as one would expect. And we know he came to the United States aboard an American troop ship: the *USS General Black.* He left Bremen, Germany and arrived in New York Harbor on May 31, 1950. With that, he served for two years in parishes in the Buffalo Diocese and, he said, "tried to learn the administration of parishes in America." The parishes, Assumption and Transfiguration, were of Polish background so the adjustment to America was not too abrupt. Yet he was still concerned with academic matters. Fr. Paczek wrote, "The Felician sisters helped me learn the English language."

CHAPTER SEVEN

To America

The movement of Fr. Paczek to America was part of a general plan of the Pallottine authorities to establish a Polish Pallottine institution in the United States. Involved were the congregation's leaders in Rome, perhaps Poland, but more immediately the superiors in France. Fr. Valerian Paczek was a key man for the project. He already had almost five years of service in the English-speaking world and was a man of proven leadership abilities. His appointment as assistant pastor in the Buffalo, New York, parishes of Assumption and Transfiguration was seen, he himself admitted, as an "acclimation" experience, a chance to learn American parish procedures and to develop a sense for the styles of leadership found among North American bishops and religious communities.

The goal was, of course, to acquire a "home base," some place to work from and to popularize the Polish version of The Society of the Catholic Apostolate way of life. The ultimate hope was to attract American men and get rooted on the New World soil.

Assisting in this endeavor was probably the fact that the order had "spare" wartime priests, who like Fr. Paczek either didn't want to return to Poland, or couldn't for political reasons. Certainly there was the possibility of sending money back to the Pallottine community in their still devastated homeland.

The fact that there already was a Pallottine priest residing at North Tonawanda, New York, made things a little easier, a "home base" was in place. Fr. V. Paczek (no longer "Germen" except when he met Home Army veterans) became rector of the new community in November 1952. His term of office was to be six years.

Plunging into the task with his usual energy, he was involved in setting up a Mission House in Buffalo and purchasing land at North Tonawanda for a chapel and possible school. In his own words he later recalled, "I was working as a missionary, giving retreats to sisters and 40-hour devotions in different parishes, working with different organizations and writing articles." In 1957 he published a book concerning the life of the revered founder of his order and detailing something of its traditions: *BL Wincenty Pallotti, Zalozyciel Stowarzyszenia Apostolstwa Katolickiego.*

Always in the back of his mind was the desire to obtain a doctorate in Canon Law. He had received his master's degree in that field from the clandestine University of Warsaw, completing it during the wartime days. Now in 1954, in the Free World, he approached the officials in what was called the Polish University Abroad, whose headquarters were in London, England. Poland, with its inhospitable Communist government, was not conducive to Catholic institutions of higher education so Polish professors, themselves in exile, ran the London-based University.

The faculty authorized Fr. Paczek's curricula proposals and, in the midst of his many pastoral duties in North Tonawanda, he began his studies. To do so he corresponded with professors, not only in London, but also in such far-flung places as Rome, Madrid, Persia, and Sweden. His nearest contact and a major support in his studies was a professor in Ottawa, Canada.

Love of learning was a mark of his whole life. Interviewing Fr. Paczek in 1977 at his parish in Mooreton, North Dakota, LuAnn Kuntz quoted him in her booklet, *Fare Thee Well:*

> A real knowledgeable person must get his research from the source, says Father. That's why he paid so much attention to language. In order to read the classics and history of long ago, he says, one must learn the language they were written in—otherwise the reader gets mussed-up information, spoiled by translation.
>
> Father's search for knowledge often takes him to the library where he has spent most of his vacations—and loves it.

The doctoral work occupied his attention in New York and subsequently in his North Dakota small town assignments. His major professors, to whom he was very grateful, were Dr. W. Mystowiski and Dr. J. Gawenda. These men guided him through the maze of international academic advisors. On January 5, 1972, the great day arrived. He was awarded his Doctorate in Canon Law. It was a degree with a European perspective, however, for in some ways it covered both civil and church law. His dissertation was published (printed and bound in European fashion) in a small volume. Many hundreds were produced and distributed. The title was *Nauczanie religii w szkolach publiezwych i udzielanie pomocy sckolom wyznaniowym wedlug ustaw w USA* ("Religious Teaching in Public Schools and Providing Help to Denominational Schools According to USA Laws").

By 1958, at North Tonawanda, there was a community of eight

Figure 23. Fr. Paczek received his doctorate in Canon Law in 1972.

priests. Two vocations, new members, were part of the group, a man from the US and one from Canada. (Fr. Paczek filed his first naturalization papers—the intent to become a citizen—in 1951. He was sworn in as a full citizen five years later.)

There was, however, a certain unrest in his soul. Perhaps it was the stress accumulated over the past twenty years: the underground, the battles, the post-war refugee responsibility, and the administrative work in his new country. Perhaps his restlessness came from tensions in the life of the new religious house. Maybe after being a highly mobile person, the life of a community became burdensome.

Fr. Paczek received advice from a friend, Fr. Joseph Mentel, the above mentioned conscripted labor priest who served under him at the German postwar camp at Lubeck. Through correspondence, Fr. Mentel said that he had met Archbishop A. Muench, Apostolic Delegate to Germany, and through the good graces of this prelate (still Bishop of Fargo) had come to North Dakota and found it to be a very hospitable part of America.

In 1958, Fr. Paczek made a tentative approach to the Fargo Diocese Auxiliary Bishop, Leo F. Dworshak. He wondered about a possible pastoral job in eastern North Dakota. Such a thing was almost commonplace in the Fargo Diocese; Archbishop Muench was instrumental in sending at least eight "displaced person" priests to North Dakota. Fr. Paczek, in his letter to Fargo, expressed his desire to do parish rather than missionary work.

The usual interchange of documents took place: permission from his Pallottine superiors, resumes, Polish documents, and recommendations. One very favorable recommendation came from Archbishop Joseph Gawlina, by this time a high-ranking Vatican official. This was the bishop exiled from Dluga 15 who had visited Fr. Paczek during his labors in the German refugee camp situations.

By January 1960, Fr. Paczek received permission to take a pastoral assignment in the North Dakota diocese for "three years." The implication was that if he so desired at the end of the time he could be released from his ties with the Pallottines and be "incardinated" (officially accepted) into the Fargo Diocese.

Figure 24. St. Boniface
Church, Lidgerwood, ND

    This was the beginning of the long and final chapter in his life. After several short stints as a substitute pastor, he was appointed to Lidgerwood, North Dakota's Bohemian Church, St. John Nepomucene, in 1963. In this parish he was well received. He gave sermons and often counseled parishioners in the Czech language. He was popular with the townspeople of all faiths. Not surprisingly, in 1968 the Bishop gave him the task of consolidating St. John's Church with Lidgerwood's larger St. Boniface (originally German) Church. He then became pastor of the combined parishes, centered at the St. Boniface facilities. For a time, too, he cared for the nearby St. Martin's Church at Geneseo.

Figure 25. St. Anthony Church, Mooreton, ND

In 1975 he took over the pastorate of the rather large (4,000 membership) St. Michael's Church in the City of Grand Forks. Here he found himself again in an administrative type of job, but it was also during the turmoil of the post-Vatican Council years. His health was, perhaps, giving him trouble, for he left the Grand Forks parish and almost immediately had a serious gallbladder problem, which left him in a near-death situation. Yet he regained his health and took a parish thirty miles northeast of Lidgerwood, the St. Anthony parish at Mooreton. North Dakota has lots of small towns, so he at the same time served St. Peter and Paul parish in Mantador.

With his retirement in 1986, after 52 years in the active priesthood, he returned to Lidgerwood to live in a little house that he had built and had carefully preserved for his golden years. He was very happy. It gave him a chance to study, to pray, to putter in his garden, and visit at a leisurely pace with his neighbors.

CHAPTER EIGHT

In Perspective

THE YEARS IN PARISHES in North Dakota's small towns seem to have been the happiest in Fr. Paczek's life. It started with his arrival in St. John Nepomucene, the Czech parish in Lidgerwood. He recalled his first moments: "Hearing hours of confessions on Saturdays, I was completely shocked, listening to English, German, Bohemian, and Polish languages. My goodness, I said, to [travel] the thousands of miles and be home again?" He never lost his amazement at the religious fervor of his people. He wrote: "All with deep faith, good heart and understanding, approaching the sacraments." These same phrases occur in his 50th Jubilee Book as he described the people he served later, not only in the churches at Lidgerwood, but also at Geneseo, Mooreton, and Mantador. This Jubilee book, ostensibly written to celebrate five decades of service, contains only a disappointing half-dozen pages about himself, but devotes twenty-five pages to the "wonderful" people who came under his pastoral care.

Busy as he was in parish work, he continued to develop his intellectual skills: he subscribed to and contributed to the support of two theological journals written by a world-wide array of Polish scholars (edited and published in London). He kept up on church scholarship with Canon Law books and the continued acquisition of dogmatic publications. (After his death, the Cardinal Muench Seminary inherited his "library").

Fr. Paczek's Doctorate in Canon Law did not go unnoticed by the Diocese of Fargo authorities. At various times he was the diocesan Tribunal's Defender of the

Bond; he was, for a while, a Vicar for Religious and was also the Promoter of Justice. Canon Law was central to his life; he peppered his official correspondence with citations from pertinent law passages.

Though far from most Polish Army veterans' centers—East Coast, Chicago, Detroit, and Los Angeles—he maintained a lively correspondence with the men who shared his personal experience in the battles and the camps. As early as 1948, while in Germany, he joined the Polish Combatants Association. In the United States he was a lifelong member of the Polish Resistance Veterans Association. He was, in fact, sometimes featured in their publication, *Bulletyn Informacyjno Historyczny.* Several times he attended their national gatherings. On September 28, 1979, in Chicago, he was an honored guest and gave the invocation at a prestigious banquet commemorating the 35th anniversary of the Warsaw Uprising. His personal papers, collected after his death, contain many

Visit to President of Polish Government in Exile (Major General T. Pelczynski) London 1966

"old friend" kind of letters from officers who led the Uprising battles.

The Polish Free Government in London—which continued in spite of being disavowed by the Warsaw Communist government—was aware of Fr. Paczek's accomplishments, both during the war and afterwards. On July 1, 1964, he was promoted to the rank of Lieutenant Colonel in the Polish Army. On November 10, 1990, the Polish President in Exile made him a full Colonel. In that same year, when the Free

Government was ready to close its doors and a non-Communist regime was being set up in Warsaw, the London President presented him with the medal: *Order of Polonia Restituta.* (The reader will find, in the last pages of this volume, a list of all the honors given to Fr. Paczek through the years.)

The American government recognized Fr. Paczek's status; in fact it recognized the status of all the Polish Uprising veterans. They were true allies during the Second World War, yet because of the Communists, they were "soldiers without a country." Fr. Paczek had full entitlement to use the U.S. Veterans Hospital facilities. (One of the sad oversights during Fr. Paczek's funeral services was the absence of an American Legion or Veterans of Foreign Wars color guard.)

Fr. Paczek traveled to London in 1966. He visited the Polish President in Exile while there. He probably also consulted with his advisors concerning his doctorate at the London-based Polish University Abroad. On two occasions he led a group of North Dakota pilgrims to the Vatican (1975 and 1984). These three trips were the only times he left America. He never returned to Poland.

In fact, he never expressed, at least in public, any nostalgia toward his homeland. Close family members were, for the most part, deceased. Some may have been casualties during the war. Poland, by the end of the hostilities, lost nine million of its citizens, either by death or exile. Fr. Paczek probably sent money to surviving family members in the very difficult immediate post-war years. He is said to have also helped with the cost of providing a suitable tombstone for his parents' graves.

His lack of nostalgia for Poland may have been due to the fact that the Warsaw he knew had been completely obliterated in 1944-1945. The nation, too, he knew was drastically changed. It was a pawn in the hands of Russia and their Communist government appointees. Fr. Paczek knew, too, that if he ever returned to Poland he would be detained, maybe even imprisoned, for, sad as it might be, he was a *persona non grata.* Perhaps for him there was no Poland to return to. His home was North Dakota and at the end of his life was his little house and yard in Lidgerwood, his garden, his memories, his prayers, and his many supportive friends.

Father Valerian Paczek died at the age of ninety-one. Several years before his death he suffered a stroke that affected his speech and his memory. His last days were at St. Gerard's Rest Home in nearby Hankinson, and it was there that he passed away. His funeral was held in Lidgerwood's St. Boniface Church on June 21, 2001. He is buried in the parish cemetery a half-mile west of the city, under the open sky, swept by the warm winds of summer and the snows of winter. It is a strange, yet fitting, resting place for a man of God who was thrust into the worst ravages of war, had seen at close hand great empires grappling in deadly combat, yet found his true happiness among kind and devout people in a rather remote part of Middle America.

His tombstone is simple, without any words of praise. His obituary in the Lidgerwood *Monitor* contained only a brief mention of his military past. "He served in the Polish Army from 1935 to 1945, and in the English Army from 1945 to 1950 as a Senior Chaplain." That's all there is in print: no mention of prisoner camps, battles, rank or medals. Yet it is the way he would have wanted it. With hindsight, we can say it summarizes his life: A priest, a soldier, and a quiet hero.

CHAPTER NINE

An Afterword

HE SELDOM SPOKE OF THE WAR. With the exception of five brief pages in his 50th Anniversary Book, it was almost as if it didn't exist. Why? Was it so painful? Perhaps. Certainly he was sensitive to his family and friends living back in Poland. Word would travel across the Atlantic and their livelihood could be jeopardized. (A family member did, on at least one occasion, warn him about using care in what he wrote and said.) When he sent letters to Poland, for example, he would at times send them first to a friend in Italy to be dispatched with no return address. Fr. Paczek was also aware that after the war the Polish government "rewrote" history. Their version of the "liberation" eliminated as much as possible references to the AK, the *Armia Krajowa,* the non-Communist underground forces. The Free Government in London did not exist. Rather the Polish Communist underground, which was relatively small in size, were the true "liberators": the *Armia Krajowa* veterans were shunted off into the sidelines, often the object of discrimination and received no honors as heroes. Fr. Paczek was probably aware that any words of his would be injurious to someone, or at least they would be ignored.

Yet in the United States and Britain, some Polish language publications were being printed in an attempt to tell the full story. In the footnotes of rather small volumes one finds a reference to Fr. Paczek, so scholars did write him, seeking his information.

Yet he was selective even in his communications. A Lidgerwood lady who often cooked a meal for him said that as he opened his mail he would read the message and sometimes destroy the papers saying, "No one should know about these matters."

Nonetheless, after three decades of Communist life in Poland, a more balanced presentation of the Uprising events began to be published, even in Poland. It was at this time that Fr. Paczek, who read almost every book and many of the articles being published, began to "speak out." Among his personal papers were found numerous copies of letters (written in the late 1970s and 1980s) in which he began to describe the war as he experienced it. It was his attempt to "set the record straight." And it was thanks to these latter-day communications, all in Polish, that the writers of this volume have been able to reconstruct at least some parts of Fr. Paczek's life. Notable among these items was a small booklet (70 pages) he published in 1989: *55 Lat W Sluzbie Bogu, Ojczyznic i Bliznim.*

Why was he afraid? Among his papers, at his death, was found a US permit to carry a concealed weapon. It had been regularly renewed and was valid until he was 86 years old. Perhaps "afraid" is the wrong word. Cautious? Alert? Yet he was on guard. Many of his parishioners knew that he had a revolver, and was known, at times, to carry it. What was behind this caution? He showed no signs of mental illness, no paranoia, as we know it. He was a person who loved people, radiated a sense of joy, loved conversation, would often sit at the piano and lead groups of friends in song.

Why, for example, did he leave Europe? He could have stayed with his fellow Pallottines in post-war France and Britain. Why did he leave New York and go to what, in the eyes of many people, is the "end of the world"; North Dakota, of all places?

There is what they call today "Post-Traumatic Stress Syndrome." Perhaps that's the answer. Neighbors did say he disliked dogs; when taking a walk he would carry a cane or a stick. One neighbor said he was deathly afraid of thunderstorms. When they occurred, "he would come to my house, go to the basement and stay there till it was over." Another neighbor said when Fr. Paczek would take his garbage out in the evening he left his back door, locked it, deposited his bag in the container, and would then unlock the door and enter his house. There were times, too, in which at night he would stretch a rope across the stairway to his second floor bedroom quarters.

Was it Post-Traumatic Stress Syndrome? Such a condition could be long lasting. Five years of working in the shadows of the Gestapo, with their torture and death procedures, would leave a deep impression. One of Fr. Paczek's fellow countrymen, a small-town priest in the Fargo Diocese, a survivor of the camp at Dachau, when answering his doorbell, would open the door a few inches, and then with recognition, welcome the visitor. And this practice was always part of his life.

Could it have been more than a deep-seated residue from the war? Was he afraid of assassination? Even the Communists had assassins at work in post-war Europe, even perhaps in the United States. Yet in perspective, Fr. Paczek, in spite of his Radio Free Europe anti-Communist broadcasts, was really a minor figure, hardly worth the effort. But maybe there was more to the picture? He was known to have carried "large sums of money" during the war. Could someone think he had appropriated some of the money and still had it in his possession? Or from another perspective, did he, perhaps, know an individual who was a "double agent" in the underground and later became prominent in the various Communist governments? If such were the case, Fr. Paczek would become an undesirable witness who should not survive. All this sounds like James Bond sort of stuff, but it still leaves us with the question: Why should a well-balanced man be afraid?

Another question? On a number of occasions, Fr. Paczek in conversation, perhaps in sermons, spoke of some mysterious events during his war years. In his 50th Jubilee Booklet he said, "I would have been killed in the war six times, but was protected by the Blessed Mother." The reader can probably find, in this volume, events that must surely be counted among the six miraculous moments. These include the two times he escaped from the Russians, the parachute drop into Poland from London, the 600 mm cannon projectile that didn't explode, the shells that burst outside the hospital when the bishop delayed him, as well as the "take cover" event with the honor guard at the church, and, of course, the surrender moments.

Miraculous events continued to happen even in America. He wrote in his 50th Jubilee Booklet:

> We must mention my short stay in Grand Forks was because of my health. Seven days after I came to Mooreton, I had a gall bladder attack, landed on the operating table for six hours, and was pronounced dead for three minutes. During this short moment, I had a vision in which I learned that Cardinal Wojtyla would be elected Pope.

This was a strange occurrence. The hospital attendants attributed his "vision" to the effects of the medications. Yet why should the name Wojtyla come to his mind? Fr. Paczek had never met him and no one in the worldwide church considered Wojtyla a serious candidate for any future papal election.

A Final Who: As mentioned earlier in this volume, at the moment of surrender, as the Home Army survivors were coming out of the rubble, a German officer (a general ?) asked Fr. Paczek about the youthful age of the combatants. Fr. Paczek said that many were college students and Boy Scouts. The officer, with tears in his eyes, spoke of his own sons (nephews ?) on the Russian front. "Will I ever see them again?" Fr. Paczek comforted the man, "Sir, everything is in God's hands. At a time like this we must have a deep faith." "Thank you, Chaplain," the officer stammered, almost in anguish.

Who was the officer? Fr. Paczek, all his life, spoke kindly of the Germans. He did often say, "Never trust a Russian." But at times he mentioned a German General whom he considered a saint, that's the word he used, "saint." Could this be the commanding general of the German forces opposing the Home Army in the Warsaw battles? Could it be none other than the SS Obergruppenfuher, Erich von dem Bach-Zelewski?

It is not only possible, it's almost certain. Polish accounts say—and photos bear this out—there was only one general, von dem Bach, with two minor officers, present at the surrender. Could von dem Bach have been a saint? Now we have a puzzle within a puzzle. Most descriptions of General von Bach describe him as a long-time Nazi party member with close ties to Heinrich Himmler. He was the man who set up the Auschwitz camp. He was in charge of anti-partisan actions in Belarus and the Ukraine. In the post-war crimes accounts he was said to have the blood of thousands of Jews and non-Jews on his hands. (By the end of 1941, 50,000 SS troops, local police, and auxiliaries were reportedly under his control. Their job was to eliminate Germany's "racial enemies.")

Yet Polish sources describe him as "kind" and displaying a genuine concern for Warsaw and all of Poland. (He was born in Polish-German Pomerania.) Polish history does detail the ways he tried to end the Warsaw hostilities, using emissaries from the civilian world, the Church, and the Red Cross. He established safe streets for civilians to leave the city without harm. He did have the vicious German General Kaminski tried and executed. Indeed, the photographs of the surrender show him receiving General "Bor" with great informality, shaking hands, without military cap and displaying none of the insignia of a conquering warrior. There is no question that he and his men treated the Home Army combatants as they emerged from the rubble with great respect. (One report says his soldiers even saluted them.) And General von dem Bach made sure they were sent off to prison camps with all the rights of the Geneva conventions.*

Could this be the same officer who was accused of atrocities in the War Crimes Trials? How does it fit together? Reading the proceedings of the Nuremberg trials, it will be noted that several times in his testimony he protested, saying he had a "conscience." A sketch of his life says that he suffered a "nervous breakdown" several years before the Warsaw Uprising. It was attributed to the violence he was witnessing. Did he have a dramatic change of heart? In the trial records he says it took a long time to divest himself from the ideology in which he was ingrained. Perhaps

*A prominent Polish historian, Stefan Korbonski, quoted von dem Bach's conversation with "Bor": "We must together try to save the magnificent soldiers of the Home Army....We Germans and you Poles shall fight against the common enemy" (the Russians).

von dem Bach saw the folly of the Nazi activities and developed a compassion for those who were suffering.

The post-war crimes trials (Nuremberg?) attributed some guilt to him but he was never executed, like some of his fellow Nazi general officers. He spent time in prison and at least ten years in house arrest (living at home). He was on trial at least two times for participating in the murder of anti-Hitler German leaders and German Communists. He is said to have written a personal autobiography. It must be a rare book. It would be interesting to read what he wrote about the Warsaw battle.

This is, indeed, the man whom Fr. Paczek considered a "saint." To continue the story further, Fr. Paczek at times said this German officer "saved my life." And that he did, if only by putting a peaceful end to the Warsaw hostilities. Here's where the story gets even stranger. Fr. Paczek said that later, "I helped save his life." How could this be? At the end of hostilities, Fr. Paczek was in a prisoner of war camp. Could it be that Fr. Paczek, a major serving later as a British post-war chaplain, sent letters to war crimes tribunals in defense of von dem Bach, testifying to the good treatment received at the Warsaw surrender process and in the ensuing disposition of the Home Army movement to German camps? It's all a series of puzzles! We'll have to wait till the next world to learn "the rest of the story."

CHAPTER TEN

Fr. V. Paczek – Medals & Awards

- *Krzyz Walecznych* (Cross of Valor) August 8, 1944

- *Zloty Krzyz Zaslugi Z Mieczami* (Gold Cross of Merit with Swords) August 18, 1944

- *Medal Wojskowy* (four times) (Army Medal—a kind of campaign ribbon) 1944, etc.

- Commendation: From General Bor Komorowski (for work with soldiers and civilians) September 15, 1945

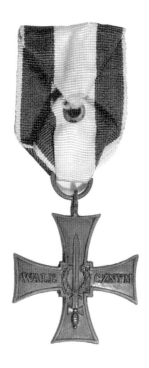  

- Commendation from British Imperial General Staff, August 9, 1949

- Member of Officer Corps, Chaplaincy, from General W. Anders, 1964

- *Krzyz Armii Krajowej* (Cross of Underground Army), 1979

- *Kazyz, Kawalerski Orderu Odrodzenia Polski* (Knight with Cross; Freedom of Poland), 1980

- Gold Medal from Association of Soldiers in Eastern Polish Armies, 1980

- Hallers Medal with Swords, 1980

- *Order Polonia Restituta,* 1990

- Commendation from Polish Veterans Groups

- Commendation for services to God, Country and Military, Boy Scouts Organization, Hanover, 1949

- Polish Combatants Association, London, December 1, 1949

Being a "non-person" in the Polish Communist post-war days, Fr. Paczek receives none of the many Peoples Republic of Poland awards.

Sources

FR. V. PACZEK left a quite extensive collection of letters, photographs, newspaper clippings, and official documents. Unfortunately he saw the various items as personal memorabilia rather than historical records. As a result the dates of composition, the salutations, and places of origin are usually missing. (The major items are also in Polish.) A researcher can however, find his collection in the Fr. V. Paczek Basic File at the Cardinal Muench Seminary Library in Fargo, North Dakota. Three of his published booklets are listed in the Bibliography of this volume: his personal *On the Golden Jubilee;* his review of the war years, *55 Lat w Sluzbie Bogo* and his chronicles of the ex-prisoners of war camps, *Duszpasterstwo Polskiego.*

The story of the German occupation of Poland can be found in numerous books. We used Richard Lukas, *Forgotten Holocaust;* Stefan Korbowski, *Polish Underground State* and *Fighting in Warsaw;* Andrew Hempel, *Poland in World War II;* and Tadeusz Bielecki, *Dodziemna Walka o Polske.* Our bibliography lists these and other pertinent volumes.

The tragic details concerning Jews in Poland and the Warsaw Ghetto have been fairly well documented. We used a variety of sources, but in the bibliography we mention Paul Halberg, *Destruction of European Jews* and Nechama Tec, *When Light Pierced the Darkness.*

The actual Uprising of 1944 is described in Adam Borkiewicz, *Powstanie Warszawskie,* in Jan Dobraczynski, *Gra w Wybijanego,* and in Norman Davies, *Uprising '44.* These and other references are listed in the bibliography.

Bibliography

A surprising amount of information on the above topics can be found at various Internet sources. Understandably, some material is valuable; some is worthless.

Finally, for the casual reader who wishes an overview of Warsaw during the Occupation years, we suggest the movie, *The Pianist*. This excellent film deals with the 1943 Jewish Uprising, but it shows the German occupation as it was experienced by every Warsaw resident. Fr. Paczek was part of it all, both as an observer, but also as a participant. Yes, even as a participant, the movie shows gunfire and violence right at the door of his Red Cross Hospital. Even more, Dr. Franciszek Raszeja received Fr. Paczek's advice and blessing-absolution before going to his death doing surgery in the ghetto. This event is mentioned in the film.

Bielecki, Tadeusz. *Podziemna Walka O Polske Niepodlegla* (Philadelphia: Nakladem Wvdawnictwa "Promyk", 1979)

Borkiewicz, Adam. *Powstanie Warszawskie* (Warszawa Instytut Wydawniczy PAX, 1964)

Brown, Alan. *Airmen in Exile* (Phoenix Mill: Sutton, 2000)

Davies, Norman. *Rising '44, The Battle for Warsaw* (London: Viking Penquin, 2004)

Dobraczynski, Jan. *Gra w Wybijanego* (Warszawa: Instytut Wydawniczy PAX, 1962)

Gruzewski, Jan and Kopf, Stanislaw. *Dni Powstania - Kronika Fotograficzna Walczacej Warszawy* (Warszawa: PAX, 1957)

Halberg, Paul. *The Destruction of the European Jews* (New York: Holms and Meier, 1985)

Hempel, Andrew. *Poland in World War II* (New York: Hippocrene Books, 2000)

Humenski, Julian. *W Sluzbie Ojczyzny* (Warszawa: Wydawnictwo Ministerstwa Obrony Narodowe, 1969)

Korbonski, Stefan. *The Polish Underground State* (New York: Hippocrene Books, 1978)

Korbonski, Stefan. *Fighting in Warsaw* (New York: Hippocrene Books, 2004)

Kuntz, LuAnn. *Fare Thee Well* (Fargo, ND: Knights of Columbus, 1978)

Lukas, Richard C. *Forgotten Holocaust: The Poles Under German Occupation, 1939-1945* (New York: Hippocrene Books, 1991)

MacKenzie, William. *Secret History of the SOE: 1940-1945* (London: St. Ermin's Press, 2000)

Orpen, Neil. *Airlift to Warsaw, the Rising of 1944* (Norman: University of Oklahoma, 1984)

Paczek, Walerian. *55 Lat W Sluzbie Bogu, Ojczynie i Bliznin* (Lidgerwood, ND: 1989)

Paczek, Walerian. *Duszpasterstwo Polskiego Okregu Wojskowego* (Wentdorf, Germany: 1946)

Paczek, Walerian. *On the Golden Jubilee* (Mooreton, ND: 1984)

Stachiewicz, Piotr. *Starowka, 1944* (Warszawa: Wydawnictow Ministerstwa Obrony Naropowej, 1983)

Tec, Nechama. *When Light Pierced the Darkness* (New York: Oxford University Press, 1986)